# FINANCIAL FREEDOM:
## *MY ONLY HOPE*

# FINANCIAL FREEDOM:
## *MY ONLY HOPE*

### The Bestselling Guide to Mastering the 'Game of Money'

Jeremiah J. Brown

ISBN: 0692942025

ISBN 13: 9780692942024

Library of Congress Control Number: 2017913438

BA publishing, Los Angeles, CA

# Dedication

*Family can be defined in many ways. I define family as a group of people united by certain convictions or a common fellowship.*

*This book is dedicated to the people whom I call family. Whether through blood or through love, you all played pivotal roles in my pursuit of financial freedom, and I am forever grateful to have you all in my life. You all know who you are!*

*To Momentum Education, which taught me the value of purpose and self-actualization. This education has been far superior to any formal education that I or my Ivy League peers ever received. I will continue to live out my contract and operate out of love and abundance.*

*Lastly, this book is dedicated to you, the reader! You are reading this book because you understand the impact that financial literacy has in shifting a culture. You will be part of a new wave of enlightened people. Passing this knowledge along will certainly shift any economically deprived community and enable it to not only survive but thrive in any economic system.*

*Financial freedom: making an income while making an impact doing what you love!*

At the back of this book you will find my ten keys to success
and survival as an entrepreneur

# Table of Contents

Dedication · · · · · · · · · · · · · · · · · · · · · · · · · · · · v

Preface · · · · · · · · · · · · · · · · · · · · · · · · · · · · xiii

Why This Book? · · · · · · · · · · · · · · · · · · · · · · · xix

Introduction The American ~~Dream~~ Lie? · · · · · · · · · · xxi


1   You're in the Game, Like It or Not · · · · · · · · · · · · · 1

2   Knowledge Is the New Money · · · · · · · · · · · · · · 14

3   Print Your Own Money—Legally · · · · · · · · · · · · 26

4   You Can Have It All · · · · · · · · · · · · · · · · · · · · · 36

5   Protect Your Assets like the Rich · · · · · · · · · · · · 48

6   Failure Is the Best Degree · · · · · · · · · · · · · · · · · 60

7   You Are Not an Island · · · · · · · · · · · · · · · · · · · · 74

8   How Financial Intelligence Creates Wealth · · · · · · · 88

9   So You Want to Be a Millionaire, Huh? · · · · · · · · · 99

10   Silver Rights · · · · · · · · · · · · · · · · · · · · · · · · · 114

11   More Than Money · · · · · · · · · · · · · · · · · · · · · 146

Final Thoughts · · · · · · · · · · · · · · · · · · · · · · · 163
For My Fellow Millennials · · · · · · · · · · · · · · · · 167
About the Author · · · · · · · · · · · · · · · · · · · · · · 183

# Preface

The time is 4:15 p.m. It is a Thursday afternoon, and my lady and I are boarding a flight heading to Turks and Caicos. She mentions how she experienced an unsettling comment earlier in the day from one of her coworkers when she boasted about taking this exciting trip to the islands.

Her colleague apparently couldn't comprehend how she was able to make such an expensive trip outside the country. So he began to ask her questions about me and my occupation. He said, "Wow, who is this interesting fellow in your life? Is he an athlete?"

She replies "No, he is not."

Her coworker then responded, "Is he a rapper?"

"No," said my lady, "he is actually in technology."

"Technology, huh…is he white?"

I share this story because there is a reason for this psychology. We live in a society that struggles to think outside the box. A society that accepts what it hears and sees as truth and cannot comprehend any possibilities or variables outside the realm of what it knows to be. It is these beliefs that paralyze civilizations and stop humanity from moving forward and evolving. These blinders are often found in the world of finance and money. We are told that money is the root of all evil, that wealthy people are greedy and selfish, and that the poor and middle classes are incompetent, lazy moochers who are responsible for their own financial and wealth shortcomings. But the truth is that there is more to the game of money than these simple beliefs and presumptions. There is an insidious and stealthy agenda that is being implemented to keep us dependent on our current monetary system to survive. Unfortunately, it is through this financial system that we determine our value, our dignity, and our self-worth, all based on how many pieces of paper we have. It amazes me how these pieces of paper, derived from trees, have the power to grant power and influence how one is perceived in this world.

# Financial Freedom: *My Only Hope*

The problem is not necessarily what we do not know but what is "wired" into our thought processes about money. Many of us have a "work hard and spend" mentality and are trained to think emotionally about money and possessions. We feel anxiety when we're unemployed, fear when we're underemployed, and even more anxiety as we climb the corporate ladder. When we hear about the markets crashing, rebounding, and then crashing again only to go back up, the anxiety grows. This ambiguity causes us to go shopping for new houses or cars, spend money at the club, or pay for entertainment to avoid this anxiety—only to have the anxiety resurface Monday morning. It is this repetitive cycle that spearheads our dependency on a game that we do not even know we are playing. This is the game of money and financial intelligence.

My path to reaching financial freedom took more than pieces of fiat paper. It took knowledge, failure, and education—real-world education, that is. Some people have many degrees and are well versed in financial theory and the principles of wealth; however, as quoted in *The Matrix*, there is a significant difference between knowing the path and walking the path. I am walking that path.

In this book, you will learn how to walk the path to financial freedom. You will discover real-world practices and concepts that will help you get a better understanding of how to increase your wealth and become financially educated, because it's sometimes the things that we don't know we don't know that impede our abilities to advance in our lives and achieve our financial goals. So let us begin this financial awakening!

*We are free to evade reality...but not free to avoid the abyss we refuse to see.*

— *AYN RAND*

# Why This Book?

You can never have too much financial education!

This is not a book about theory or the philosophy behind becoming rich. This book is about real-world application and proven results. You will get the same real-world financial education that people of affluent backgrounds get from birth. This book will provide the kind of information that creates generational wealth, dynasties, and multimillionaires. As I wrote this book, I wanted to write it for someone like me—an ordinary person who wants to live an extraordinary life! Someone who came from poverty, who struggles to thrive in this economy, and who wants to learn why 1 percent of the population owns more wealth than the bottom 99 percent (you and I). I had to retrain my mind to think like the wealthy to begin my journey of wealth building. It is now your turn. If you want to learn how to master the game of money, then this book is for you.

Since your birth, a fairy tale has been recycled, telling you that if you work hard, save money, go to school, and do the right thing, you will be rewarded financially and have a shot at success. However, all we seem to experience is a lifetime of debt, financial losses, and corruption in the system, all while witnessing nepotism rewarding the people who otherwise would not be able to compete with us. We watch athletes, entertainers, hedge-fund managers, college dropouts, and the traditionally uneducated accumulating massive amounts of wealth while standing on our backs to climb the money tree. We work hard to fund their lives and pay them the money we worked hard for so that we can get their disrespect and a slap in the face if we don't agree with them. Is this fair? I don't think so, but it is the system we live in. My job is to help you learn the game and play it better than anyone else. Are you up for the challenge?

# Introduction

## The American ~~Dream~~ Lie?

America is still a land of opportunity, isn't it? A place where anyone can make it to the top if willing to work hard and aspire to reach greatness. However, imagine that you are playing a game of Monopoly. You arrive to the game only to find out that all the money has already been divided up and all the property has already been bought, but you are told that you have the same opportunity as anyone else to win and it is your fault if you don't. Will you not be playing in a rigged game?

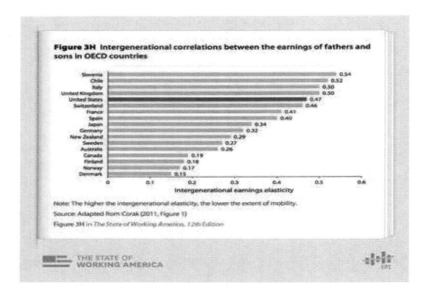

**Figure 3H** Intergenerational correlations between the earnings of fathers and sons in OECD countries

Note: The higher the intergenerational elasticity, the lower the extent of mobility.

Source: Adapted from Corak (2011, Figure 1)

Figure 3H in *The State of Working America, 12th Edition*

THE STATE OF WORKING AMERICA

Economic mobility is terrible in the United States.*

I know many of us want to know what the hell is going on in the world today. All of a sudden, the world doesn't feel like the one our parents and grandparents grew up in. That was a world in which people could bootstrap their way to wealth without higher education, expensive degrees, financial literacy, or resources. They could achieve the American dream with just good old hard work, ambition, and persistence.

The growing gap between the wealthy and everyone else has been the greatest moral issue of our time. This is more of a crisis of virtues and values than it is a financial one. The introduction of our current debt-based monetary system, along with globalization and racial economic inequality, has been beneficial to one side of our economy, the rich, and has been devastating to the poor and middle class. Globalization and automation have destroyed thousands of blue-collar jobs, all the while cutting costs for the founders of corporations, enriching them, and cutting access to wealth accumulation for the average person. Racial economic inequality has forced a group of people out of this wealth-creation game altogether, making them the lowest income group with the highest unemployment rates and lowest graduation and ownership rates in the world. What makes matters worse is the rise of the "gig" economy, in which people are forced to take lower wages due to an influx of workers forced to take this route. Corporations don't have to hire as many people as they used to anymore; they can just outsource work or even automate their business models using AI (artificial intelligence) systems. In my opinion, if the wealth disparity continues, it will destroy the American dream, the ambition and hope people have to claw their way to the top, and create a larger dependence on the government for help and financial assistance.

The American dream today is a hoax. Ironically, the American dream is what keeps the economy going. This idea spurs innovation, creates jobs, and orchestrates the illusion of wealth. The more belief we have in the system, the longer the system can thrive. But once the largest slice of the pie is given to a few people, the poor and financially deprived will lose faith in the system and revolt. This is a societal nightmare; it can spell the end to any regime if the people operating inside it start to fight with each other. How can we continue to be a global force if we are feuding among ourselves? As Jay-Z says, "Nobody wins when the family feuds." America, once a world power, will not continue to thrive if its people are divided and disconnected. This book will teach you not only about the game you are playing that you don't know you're playing, but about how we all can play it and win. This game can be a win-win scenario for us all. However, we have to work together to accomplish this. So continue to educate yourself and read this book. It *will* change your life and our society for the better. I would bet my life on it!

*We need to understand that in our current monetary system, wealth is not lost or stolen…it is simply transferred. There are winners and losers in this game of money. However, this game is often played for keeps.*

# You're in the Game, Like It or Not

**WE DON'T KNOW WHAT WE DON'T KNOW.**

I remember my mother telling me as a child that money doesn't grow on trees. The truth is, she was right. Our modern banking system creates currency far faster than trees can grow! Most of us don't even have a clue how money is created in our society. We have these financial experts, bankers, and economists using gaudy and elaborate terms like *quantitative easing* or *leverage* to make it seem more complex than it is. So what I am going to do for you in this chapter is strip the game of money down to its basic form. I am going to make it simple for you to see what game we are in and what role we play in it. It is unfortunate that this game is often dealt in fraud, deceit, and stealth. But like the late and great 2Pac said, "Once you get an understanding of the game, and what the levels and the rules of the game are, then the world is no longer a trick, but a game to be played." Let's get started...

## DEFICIT SPENDING: BMF

Every central bank around the world creates currency in much the same way we do here in the United States, but I am going to focus on the United States, as many of the world's currencies are tied to ours here. The game starts when a politician or government official promises you that in exchange for your vote, he or she will give you all the money, entitlements, and free stuff that you desire. But we all know nothing is free in this life, don't we? So to provide that "free lunch," our country spends more than its income. If you and I did that, it would be called foolish, ignorant, and reckless, right? When the government does this, it is called "deficit spending." I call it "blowing money fast."

## GLORIFIED IOUS

To pay for this "deficit spending," our Treasury creates bonds. Yes, the same bond that your grandparents buy for you as a gift on your seventh birthday with their Social Security checks is the bond that the Treasury issues. But what the hell is a bond? Other than a nice-looking check of $5,000 that will grow to $5,003 by the time you're twenty-five, a bond is a glorified IOU. It's a contract that says, "If you loan me a trillion dollars today, I will promise over a ten-year period to pay you back that money plus interest." It gets even better. Do you know those mysterious numbers you see in New York financial jumbotrons that never seem to stop increasing? Well, let me make it simple for you: Treasury bonds are our national debt. This means that you, me, our kids, and our kids' kids will all have to pay for these IOUs that the Treasury issues through future taxation. So, long story short, when our government issues a bond, it is stealing money and prosperity from our future children so that it can spend it today.

## DEBT DEALERS: BANKS

The Treasury then sells our national debt to the largest bankers in the world through a shell game called bond auctions. You are going to hear the word "bank" a lot throughout this process of currency creation, because the banks profit through every step of this cycle. The banks then sell some of these bonds to our Federal Reserve at a profit. The banks are granted the right to sell out national debt to the Federal Reserve through what is known as open market operations.

## COUNTERFEIT CHECK SCAM: FEDERAL RESERVE

The Federal Reserve buys these bonds (IOUs) from those large banks with a counterfeit check that has no money in it. This would be considered fraud if you and I were doing it, because it is drawn on an account that always has a zero balance. If you think that I am lying, here is a quote right from the horse's mouth: The Boston Federal Reserve.

> *When you or I write a check, there must be sufficient funds in our account to cover the check, but when the Federal Reserve writes a check, there is no new deposit on which that check is drawn. When the Federal Reserve writes a check, it is creating money.*

> —*"PUTTING IT SIMPLY," BOSTON FEDERAL RESERVE.*

The Fed then gives the check to the banks, and *poof*! Currency is created. The banks then take that money and buy more bonds, and the cycle is repeated in perpetuity (forever). In other words, the Federal Reserve and the Treasury are creating money out of thin air, issuing IOUs in the form of bad checks and bonds, and using the banks as middlemen to create currency. This process enriches the banks involved and indebts our society (you and me) by raising the national debt due to these IOUs that have to be paid back by us through taxation.

**Side note:** Who or what is the Federal Reserve?

Can you spot the similarities?

versus

The Federal Reserve or "the Fed" is as federal as the mailing company Federal Express (FedEx). The Federal Reserve is simply a private central bank with shareholders. These mysterious shareholders represent a percentage of ownership in this corporation, and they are entitled to an annual dividend of 6 percent. Yes, the Federal Reserve has owners, and these owners take 6 percent of the nation's income ($18 trillion in 2016) every single year just by owning the Federal Reserve. Man, I can only imagine their net worth!

## MONEY VERSUS FIAT CURRENCY

When the average person hears the word "fiat," he or she automatically thinks of an Italian automobile company that was acquired by Chrysler. But if you change the context to economic terms, the meaning of the word becomes esoteric. The word derives from a Latin origin and means "let it become" or "it shall be." In other words, fiat currency is legal tender that is backed by the government's promise—and we all know how good the government is at keeping its promises.

To the financially uneducated, money and currency may seem similar due to the perceived notion of purchasing power and medium of exchange: you can buy things with both. However, there is one significant difference between money and currency: money always has to be a store of value. This means that money has to maintain its purchasing power over long periods of time. Before 1971, the US dollar was nothing but a receipt or a "claim check" for gold. It was a representation for real money of intrinsic value—the gold and silver that was held under a deposit in the Treasury. You could trade in your currency (say, thirty dollars) and get back the equivalent (thirty dollars) in real gold or silver. But after 1971, this currency became a receipt on an IOU, that bond. Debt simply backs our monetary system. Fiat currency allows governments to print more money than we can pay back, creating cycles of boom and bust economies.

## FRACTIONAL-RESERVE BANKING

This may shock you, but when you deposit your money into the bank, you are actually loaning the bank your money. If you think that you are depositing it into an account to be safely held in trust for you, you are sorely mistaken! Within certain legal parameters, the banks can pretty much do anything they want. They can do things like loan your money out, speculate (gamble) in the stock market, and make a profit from leveraging your money.

## FRACTIONAL-RESERVE LENDING

This is where we enter the twilight zone in modern banking. Fractional-reserve lending enables banks to reserve a fraction of your deposit and lend out the rest of your money. For example, let's say I deposit $1,000 into the bank. The bank has the legal authority to lend out 90 percent of my deposit, or $900, leaving me with a 10 percent reserve amount at $100, just in case I want to take out some money. My account will still show $1,000, but that is because the bank left IOUs called "bank credit" to cover the money it took from me to lend out to someone else looking for a loan to purchase something. Since the bank credits me the $1,000 and loans out the other $900, there is now $1900 of new currency in existence. The borrower then takes the $900 that were taken from my account and buys something with it. The seller receives that $900 and deposits that money into his or her bank account, and his or her bank loans 90 percent of that and leaves "bank credit" in its place. Now there is over $2,700 in existence!

## TRUE CAUSE OF INFLATION

This process, backed by only $1,000 in vault cash (the initial deposit by me), repeats and repeats forever, expanding the currency supply and increasing the overall debt load. Some banks even have a zero reserve requirement (meaning that they can lend out all of our money deposited)! I've used simple numbers to explain how currency is created in the banking system. In reality, the money created by the banks is far greater than the figures I used in my example. In fact, 92–96 percent of all currency in existence is created by our banks! Only 3–5 percent of all currency is created by our government. The more currency we have, the more prices rise. This is called inflation. The actual definition of inflation is simply an expansion of the currency supply. The rising prices are merely an indicator of the expanding supply.

Here is a quote from the Federal Reserve acknowledging the effects of inflation:

> *The decrease in purchasing power incurred by holders of money due to inflation imparts gains to the issuers of money.*

> —*Federal Reserve*

Due to our current debt-based monetary system, inflation creates a slow and insidious tax that causes our purchasing power to dwindle over time. This is why a house in a metropolitan area that was bought for $300,000 in 1990 is worth $1,000,000 or more today. It has not increased in value; your purchasing power has decreased (it takes more money to buy that same house today than it did twenty-seven years ago).

## WE GIVE CURRENCY ITS VALUE

I hope you have a better understanding of how money is created in our society and what role we play in its creation. Our entire currency supply is nothing but numbers created out of thin air and backed by your ability to pay it back through taxation. In other words, these numbers represent our ideas, labor, and effort. We give currency its value! This money is taxed so that it can return to its original owners within the Federal Reserve with money that was created out of thin air—not a single penny was used to back this currency creation. There is a reason why income tax was created in 1913, the same year as the Federal Reserve, after all. Unfortunately, fiat debt is and will always be an intrinsic part of our financial economy.

> *"Tax dollars are needed for the Federal Reserve to create more dollars."*

> - ROBERT KIYOSAKI

**Question:** If every dollar in existence is owed back with interest, what would happen if we all stopped borrowing money? The answer to this question is simple: our economy would collapse. There is a payment due on every dollar in existence. Therefore, the entire system is finite and will come to an end one day. You just have to learn how to play the game and make it work for you, because when this game of musical chairs finally comes to a halt, you want to be the person who has a seat!

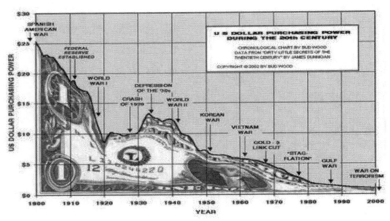

Federal Reserve Career Stat Sheet

The Federal Reserve is responsible for the following:

- One Great Depression
- Forty-three recessions

- More than 97 percent of currency value depreciation
- Trillions in bailouts (welfare for the rich)

Let's put it in terms we understand. If you are a professional athlete or a recording artist looking for a contract increase or advance or to sell a record label, the first thing that the executives check is your track record, or "proven history." In other words, "What have you done in the past and present that justifies why you are needed?" If you are a recording artist, it goes like this:

- When was the last time you produced a hit record?
- What are your streaming sales?
- How popular are you?
- How much revenue will you produce for us?

If you are a professional athlete, the executives would most likely want to know this:

- What is your usage rate?
- How many tickets can you sell? What are your endorsements? What is your marketability, likeness, and so on?
- More importantly, what are your career statistics?

If these are the questions that determine whether an individual or entity is rewarded or not, then the Federal Reserve should abide by these same standards. However, it is too powerful to subject itself to something as precarious as selling its worthiness to the public or even having a public election to elect the right candidates to serve on the reserve board. No, instead the 'Fed' politics itself and appoints people through nepotism and cronyism.

## THE FEDERAL RESERVE CAN BE YOUR ALLY

Listen, if the Fed is going to strong-arm its way into our society and we continue to allow it to, my advice to you is that you play by its rules. Playing by its rules will help you become financially free. In order to achieve financial freedom, you must understand the game you are in, master it, and identify how the Federal Reserve can be your ally. The more the Fed continues to print currency, the more assets you can leverage via debt and the less your taxes will be. Play the game, and have fun doing it! You are not going to die if you are losing, but you will start to live when you start playing the game for fun and winning. Change your perspective, and start playing the game of money like a sport!

I think by now you know how the Federal Reserve can create boom and bust economies just by printing money and lowering and raising interest rates. This is how it controls your money and its perceived value. The more it prints, the less buying power you have. Whether the Federal Reserve decides to raise or lower interest rates, you can stay ahead of the curve by reading what to do below. Here are the results of any Federal Reserve move and how you can benefit from any Fed increase or decrease in interest rates.

Lower interest rates mean the following:

- Increase in inflation
- Increase in asset prices (home values, stock market, etc.)
- Ability to leverage debt to increase your wealth
- Creation of bubbles that you can bet against
- Ability to make money with cash-flow-producing properties

Higher interest rates mean the following:

- Deflation
- Decrease in asset prices, or a "correction"
- Stocks, bonds, and real estate all on sale
- Applicability of the "buy low, sell high" model
- Ability to make money with cash-flow-producing properties

# 2

## Knowledge Is the
## New Money

In the decades following World War II, the economic pie appeared to be extremely fair. Income gains were shared by everyone, with the largest portions of income going to 90 percent of the population. This equitable economic distribution created what is known as "the middle class." But after 1971, something changed. The bottom 90 percent saw its gains get completely consumed by the 1 percent. By 2016, a little over four hundred of the richest people in America controlled more wealth than 150 million people in the country. This phenomenon shifted globally as well, having similar economic disparity statistics throughout all parts of the world.

Many people today believe debt is evil, money is controversial, and a little economic uncertainty signals a recession.

However, I believe that is not always the case. These beliefs are mainly due to a lack of financial knowledge along with manipulative rhetoric that is passed through the media to keep us dependent on "experts" (or salesmen) to handle our money. But if you are financially educated or reading this, you will quickly see how knowledge is the new money.

## 1971: KNOWLEDGE BECOMES THE NEW MONEY

Knowledge became the new form of money after 1971, when former president Nixon took the US currency off the gold standard. Before 1971, the dollar was backed by gold and silver, which guarded us against uncontrollable inflation, debt, and the rising prices of everyday goods and services. But once Nixon took us off the gold standard (without permission from Congress or us), it gave the Federal Reserve and Treasury power to print money uncontrollably throughout the world. So what is going on today is the dollar is becoming toxic; it's going down in value as the Fed prints more and more of it. I laughed sarcastically when I discovered this, because I wasn't even born in 1971. This information proved how I and everyone in my community were pretty much screwed from birth. It is more important to understand this history now than ever before because the rules of money changed after this move.

*Saving is for suckers.*

—*Damon Dash*

Those of you who did not watch the *Breakfast Club* interview with tycoon and mogul Damon Dash missed how he spoke about the philosophy and financial illiteracy behind the age-old advice of "Save your money." He used his infamous flair and passion to explain the reason why people will never get ahead in life by simply saving. I am going to clean it up a bit and explain why he is on to something here:

Allow me to go back again, most people will advise you to "save money." However, money is no longer money after 1971. So today, when bonds are paying almost zero and the Federal Reserve is printing trillions of dollars in fiat currency, pitching the notion of "saving money" is terrible advice. Since our government can mandate the amount of money that can be printed, every dollar you save becomes subjected to government control. As more money is printed, your dollar decreases in purchasing power and the money you have in the bank becomes worthless over time. As the dollar loses value every time more money is printed, saving is a sure way to let the government and banks take your money through inflation and taxes.

*Don't just save to save. Save to invest!*

—*Angela Vega*

Unfortunately, many of us are still only saving, and it is now the worst time to save. Using debt to buy assets that pay you positive cash flow can increase your wealth. Remember, you can buy assets like gold, real estate, businesses, and stocks and still lose money. Just doing and buying these things will not make you rich, but knowledge and financial literacy will. A real investor and a financially educated person can make money when the economy is up and can make even more money in a bad economy. The 99 percent of the population is consistently being taught to either save money or buy, hold, and pray that the money invested will grow over time. If this were great advice, then 99 percent of the population wouldn't be financially dependent upon the 1 percent. This constant cognitive reinforcement while expecting different results can be considered a form of insanity.

## THE SPEED OF MONEY

Today, you can make money at a rate that our parents' and grandparents' generations could only dream about. You see this in the emergence of twenty-somethings earning millions and billions using the Internet as a tool to create exponential wealth, all while their parents are still trying to make $40,000–50,000 a year. This rapid formation of wealth comes through platforms such as websites, apps, social media, and other digital forms. So the speed of producing data, information, and services has gone up to extreme levels unseen by our parents and grandparents.

Another reason why there is a huge wealth disparity between the wealthy and the poor and middle class also has to do with the velocity of money. The poor and middle class invest their money in the following ways:

- By saving
- Using stagnant investment vehicles like 401k's or pension plans.
- By dumping money into the house that they own and occupy.

The wealthy, however, do the following:

- Acquire assets
- Pull their initial investment out of those assets, without selling the assets
- Buy more assets with that same money, rather than park it and retiring their money like the poor and middle class.
- The wealthy investor keeps their money moving and increases their velocity of investing.

Retiring your 'savings' vs. Velocity of money:

Income that you retire into investments typically requires a capital gains tax once it is time to sell. When the wealthy invest their money via debt, they can use the same cash and increase their asset column tax-free, because it is debt based capital at work. The wealthy can acquire assets, like real estate, which pays them cash flow from renting out the unit. Then, through a refinance or HELOC, they receive their initial capital back and repeat the steps all over again, decreasing their tax liability, and increasing the velocity of their wealth and income.

## MONEY HAS ITS LANGUAGE; LEARN IT

When you and I take courses in school, one of the many requirements is to learn a language like Spanish, French, or Mandarin. But there is not an option to learn the language of money. Why is that? Wait! Before you correct me, allow me to explain. Language is simply vocabulary, and money has its own vocabulary. So when someone says, "It takes money to make money," that is simply not true. It takes *words*. When I invest in real estate, I am using a different vocabulary than when I am investing in the stock market or building a technology start-up.

For example, when I am looking at a property in real estate, a term that I would commonly use is "cap rate." When I am building a tech start-up, another common name I'd hear would be "valuation" or "scale." In stocks, common terms would be "P/E" and "price to book."

If you don't speak the same language as the people within these industries, it is the equivalent of you speaking Japanese in America. In other words, it would be challenging to communicate and win in that particular space.

## PREPARE FOR A DEFLATION OR HYPERINFLATION

There were two kinds of historical and notable economic depressions that happened in the world. We all know about the Great Depression, but there was also a Zimbabwe depression, an example of what is known as hyperinflation. Zimbabwe faced a terrible financial crisis and began printing so much money that a citizen had to pay one million dollars in Zimbabwe currency for a stick of gum! Stories were going around about how the people of Zimbabwe would carry around wheelbarrows of cash and would get robbed for only the wheelbarrows. The cash was too worthless even to steal. It looks like right now the United States is heading down a similar path with its massive printing of debt-based money. Knowledge is the best defense to combat any of these inevitable fates. If you think that the United States will continue to print fiat currency, you should have one strategy. If you think Janet Yellen, our current Federal Reserve chair, will take her hands off of the switch and continue to raise interest rates, you should have another strategy.

I don't know about you, but I don't have a million dollars for gum. So I am preparing heavily for this by converting my cash into an asset that pays me a dividend or cash flow. I like the real-estate play for hyperinflation because real estate is a hedge against inflation, meaning that real estate soaks up expanding currency like a sponge does water, and I can leverage debt. For most people, debt is considered a curse word, but if you're smart, you can use debt as leverage to get rich. This is why knowledge is the new money. It can prepare you to be proactive and take control of your finances rather than hope that your broker, advisor, or 401(k) and pension plan will save you if these catastrophes happen.

## SO WHY IS THE STOCK MARKET UP?

The reason why the stock market is up exponentially right now is that interest rates are low and bond markets are paying zero. There are tons of money sitting on the sidelines with no place to go, so people are being forced to invest in higher-risk instruments such as the stock market to get a better return on their money. Corporations are also inflating the stock exchange through stock buybacks (buying their stock) using debt, along with buying other companies with borrowed cash (debt). The printing of money, I believe, is corporate welfare for the rich. It's free money that allows large multinational corporations to leverage debt to monopolize industries through mergers and acquisitions.

And they say that the 99 percenters are the moochers. Give me a break!

## IGNORE YOUR IGNORANCE

To actually understand the language of money and how to stay ahead of the curve, you must ignore your ignorance about money and retrain your mind to see the other side of the coin. If you are part of the 99 percent of the population that has to share less than 40 percent of the wealth generated within our economy, then everything you have been taught about money is keeping you from reaching financial freedom. The information that is currently being spread throughout the masses tells us that "debt is bad," that we should "work for money," or that we should "focus on saving or paying down debt." However, this advice will only keep you in the rat race and dependent on the government. Breaking free of these invisible chains and financial slavery will require more than just having a salary, pension, and 401(k). You will need to understand how you can use the liquidity you have to buy assets that appreciate and pay you while you wait. The truth is we all can make money, but only a few of us can reach financial freedom and wealth. Arriving at this plateau takes not only knowledge but a burning desire to become free from economic deprivation and the ability to see and leverage both sides of the economic coin (income and debt).

## DON'T BUY THE RIGHT STOCKS; BUY STOCKS THE RIGHT WAY

> *I will tell you the secret to getting rich on Wall Street.*
> *You try to be greedy when others are fearful. And you*
> *try to be fearful when others are greedy.*

> *-- WARREN BUFFETT*

It never ceases to amaze me how the masses only think of one way that they can profit from buying shares—if stocks are going up. Learning how to profit from downward movements is just as important as the rallies within the stock market. You will never be late to the investment party if you understand this simple strategy. If you think stocks have reached their peak and you are afraid to jump in and invest, looking for stocks that are overvalued and "shorting" them can be the remedy that you need to relieve your fear and skepticism. There will always be stocks that are ready to move higher or lower, regardless of any bull or bear market run. Instead of doing what the masses are taught to do, which is to jump in when the market is rallying and run away to sell when there is a pullback or collapse, doing the opposite will give you the significant gains you need to survive any market you are in. Remember, it is not stocks that will make you rich; it is knowledge along with timing that will.

**Hint:** Look for stocks with a price-to-earnings ratio (P/E) trading no higher than fifteen times their earnings. This stock's current price should trade no more than two times its book value, and its financials (income statement, balance sheet, cash flow statement) should be as such:

**Income statement:** Positive net profit
**Balance sheet**: Positive net equity
**Cash flow statement:**
- Operating net cash flow: positive
- Investment activities: negative
- Financing activities: negative

These numbers almost always reflect the current market price of the stock. If it fails to meet the above criteria, short it using options. This will reduce your downside and increase your profit if or when the stock corrects itself.

# 3

# Print Your Own Money—Legally

## BE THE FEDERAL RESERVE

I think by now we know how the Federal Reserve can create money out of nothing and print its way to wealth. There are many ways that you can begin to print money out of nothing and become your own Federal Reserve. You can do this through owning stocks, commodities, and real estate, by selling a product or starting your own business, and through technology. Here are a few examples of how I was able to print money out of thin air just as the Federal Reserve does.

## PRINT MONEY IN TECH

Let me share with you how I can print money legally using technology. A month after my twenty-first birthday, I created a mobile app called Cyclone HD. It was a straightforward application and was designed to increase hand-eye coordination for the user. Similar to the arcade game that you see at Dave and Busters, the light would rotate around the cylinder and a user had to hit the light once it lands on the Jackpot. The initial cost to build the app was $1,500, which included programming and design. It was a free app that was available in both the Android and App store (at the time, an annual membership on those platforms cost about $150), but I incorporated in-app purchasing, which brought in revenue on the back end. Within about two months, I was able to recoup my initial investment, and from there, the printing press began. I later raised a combined total of $75,000, giving me an infinite return, as there was no more money invested into it after recovering my initial investment. The ultimate method of printing your own money in tech is through an IPO, or initial public offering. This gives you the ability to raise funds via the stock market from everyday people looking to invest in the next big thing. I don't know about you, but I'd personally rather own the company I am investing in, than give my money to someone else's company hoping for a decent return.

## PRINT MONEY IN REAL ESTATE

When I purchased my first cash-flowing property in Delaware, I initially used $12,500 as a down payment toward the unit.

This down payment represented 20 percent of the purchase price of the home. The bank was able to cover the remainder of the cost. The bank and I became partners. Now, with this money invested into the tenant-occupied unit, I immediately started receiving a positive cash flow of $275, which was profit after the mortgage, utilities and other expenses were paid from my tenant's rent. A few months later, when interest rates dropped, I refinanced the property and received all of my initial investment capital back plus an extra $550. Now, after the refinance, the cash flow decreased from $275 to about $200, but did I care? Hell no! I was making $200 every month with no money invested into the property. With the bank as a partner and without having any of my money in this investment, I was able to produce an infinite return. These are some of the secrets of the game that rarely get exposed. Leveraging debt that other people are covering while getting positive cash flow is the name of the game.

**Side note:** If you lack sufficient credit or are unemployed but have a lump sum of cash, you can still acquire property through the following strategies.

1.  You could go through an option known as seller financing. This is where the seller acts as the bank, and you

pay the seller a mortgage instead of paying the bank. You still own the title, but the seller has a lien against the title until the mortgage is paid off (the same as if you went through the bank). This benefits the seller because the seller isn't subjected to the hefty capital gains tax and can collect a fixed income and charge interests, as opposed to having a one-time lump sum that would be taxed. I only recommend that you do this if the property is owned free and clear (paid off—which 30 percent of all homes in the United States are). This is because if the sellers have the mortgage with the bank and if you miss any payments or if the seller does not pay back the mortgage, the bank can technically foreclose on the property, leaving both you and the seller out of a property.

2.  You can find homeowners who are struggling to pay their mortgage and who are in default. You offer to pay to relive them of the financial burden by proposing to pay the back payments that they owe on their mortgage and give them extra cash in their pocket in exchange for the owner to deed you the home.

An example would look like this:

Owner owns a property at $200,000. The owner has paid to date $100,000 toward the principal of the property. However, due to a job loss or economic hardship, the owner owes $15,000 on the property, and as a result of not paying it, he is in default. This is when you step in. You offer owner $30,000, which would cover the owner's debt and put cash back into his pocket, in exchange for him transferring the title or deed to you. If the owner agrees, you now own a $200,000 home for $30,000, and you have instant equity of $85,000 which included the original $100,000 the owner paid down on the mortgage, minus the $15,000 that you paid toward the owner's debt.

This is an advance strategy, and I recommend that you consult your real estate agent and attorney for more information. But this is another creative strategy to get into the real estate game.

## PRINT MONEY IN STOCKS

I hate derivative investing. Derivative investing is pretty much the following: margin calls (borrowing on short-term credit to trade), trading options, shorting stocks, foreign exchange, futures, commodity, and penny stocks. These tactics and strategies require a ton of expertise and failure to master. You will get wiped out in the market with this type of investing, because you will be a small fish in this game. This is due to flash trading and juggernaut hedge funds shifting the market with just a few trades at rapid speed. Personally, I'd rather go to the casino than invest like this in the stock market. I've made a ton of money and lost an equal amount doing so. So I will show you how to print money in the market the safe way—if there is a safe way.

Since 73 percent of the market's returns over the last forty years have come from dividends and not capital appreciation, I don't own a single security that doesn't pay a dividend. I invest in stocks that pay me a consistent monthly or quarterly dividend that is trading at or under book value with P/E ratios at no more than fifteen. This means that I look for stocks that are trading at a price no more than fifteen times its annual earnings. If a stock is trading more than two times higher than its book value or more than fifteen times its P/E ratio, this indicates a bubble, and we have all seen what happens to bubbles. They burst. I then leverage my dividend income to buy more dividend-paying stocks, compounding my total returns.

**Real-world example:** I came across a stock called (O) Realty Income Trust. This stock was a REIT (real estate investment trust) that was considered "Armageddon proof," according to CNBC. This company invested in land and had large commercial properties leasing its lands, such as Walgreens, Dollar General, Taco Bell, General Electric, and many more. The financials were the best I've seen from a REIT. It had a positive income statement and balance sheet and a sufficient cash flow statement. The price of the stock at the time was at $28 a share and had a P/E ratio of ten (this means that the stock was trading at ten times its annual income, which is not bad at all). It was also trading at about $2 under its book value, which means that in the event the company goes belly up, it will still have enough cash on its books to pay investors back their initial investment. After analyzing the numbers, I invested $3,000 into it. With the dividend income I received from the stock, I used the money to invest in other stocks. I was able to print money from my $3,000 and use that money to print more money by acquiring other stocks that paid dividends. I don't think that I will ever sell my (O) shares. For me, as long as I can get free money from it to buy other dividend-paying stocks, I will always be able to print currency. I guess the stock is Armageddon proof after all.

## OTHER WAYS TO PRINT YOUR OWN MONEY

There are so many ways to print your own money out of thin air just as the Federal Reserve does. Here are other industries and markets that will allow you to print your own money:

# Financial Freedom: *My Only Hope*

- **Intellectual property**—leveraging your knowledge of a particular subject and earning money sharing your knowledge
- **Derivatives**—options trading
- **Sneakers and clothes**—buying high-end shoes on release date and selling them after market for more than what you initially bought them for
- **Handbags, dresses, jewelry**—selling or renting out these items
- **Write a book**—writing and self-publishing your book and earning royalties from your sales
- **Entertainment industry**—being a rapper, singer, actor, director, producer or founding a record label
- **Automobiles**—flipping cars (buying an undervalue car and selling it for more)
- **Party**—throwing parties and charging enough to recoup your initial investment plus a profit
- **Start a podcast**—providing great content and thereby gaining a loyal enough audience that you can advertise your merchandise or get paid to endorse someone else's
- **Collaborative consumption**—taking advantage of the sharing economy and making money leveraging your personal items (Uber, Turo, Bezelhub, Rent-therunway, Lyft)

If you are also able to come up with a few other ways to print your own money from nothing, write them down here:

1. _____

2. _____

3. _____

## MONEY IS AN IDEA

There is a reason I am saying you can print money out of thin air just as the Federal Reserve does. This is because of the simple concept that money is an idea. It is not real. The real asset is your ability to think and create value for yourself and others. The human mind is capable of things unimaginable to the naked eye. You need to understand your fundamental knowledge, as it allows you to manifest anything you dream about. You also should know that using your ability to create value can be effortless and can require no money. Yes, we are all subject to financial barriers that siphon human growth, innovation, and evolution, but as much as they hold us back, they also create opportunities to build value for ourselves and others. I created my own way of printing money with little to no investment capital, and so can you. You can follow my model or create your model. But always remember that money isn't real. The only real thing is your imagination! Now use it, and start printing your own money—legally, of course.

# 4

# You Can Have It All

## DON'T LIVE BELOW YOUR MEANS

We often hear financial pundits and industry experts pitching the notion of "living below your means" as a form of financial intelligence and economic survival. Many of the people who practice these theories are still saddled with high-interest debt, the high cost of living, education, and healthcare, and everyday expenses that are necessary for survival. How can ordinary people live within their means when even their "means" are expensive? This is all while the wealthiest people in the world spend millions of dollars on lavish items, what I refer to as "shiny things," such as luxury yachts, planes, jewelry, and cars. I have a theory about this advice—they want to make their audience complacent. Why would you want to aspire for more when you are taught subconsciously to live a basic life? The objective for that kind of advice, in my opinion, is to suppress your inner gifts and keep you in this spinning cycle of dependency on the system. I will show you how I can avoid practicing this advice and instead expand my means.

## YOU CAN PURCHASE THAT BMW...BUT FIRST, BUY THE ASSET

I don't know about you, but I like "shiny things," and I want to experience them without a "hopefully one day" mentality. So I began to expand my means rather than live below them. I will give you an example of how I was able to do this.

I saw a BMW that I wanted online. The price was $25,000, and it required me to put $8,000 down on payments totaling $300 a month. I told myself that I would get the "shiny thing," which was the BMW. But first, I would purchase an asset (in this case, property) that would create enough cash flow to cover the monthly cost of the car. I then researched tenant-occupied properties that required a similar down payment but would pay me a positive cash flow of $300 a month after all expenses were paid. I was able to purchase a property in Vegas, and two months later (through a refinance), I took the initial money that I had used to buy the property out and bought the BMW. The property that I purchased more than covered the note on the BMW.

## Here is an illustrative example of my deal:

Total cost:               $25,000

Initial investment: $8,000 (*will lose this due to depreciation*)

**Cash *going out* of your pocket (monthly):** -$300 expense

Total cost:               $55,000

# Financial Freedom: *My Only Hope*

Initial investment: $8,000 (*equity that you can get back via refinance*)

## Cash *coming in* your pocket (monthly): +$300 income

## TRANSACTION:

- Receive my cash back using debt (that tenant pays for): $8,000
- Use the cash as a down payment for my BMW
- The $300 per month car note is paid using the cash flow from my rental property
- Rinse and repeat!

In applying this practical but brilliant method, I now had an asset that covered my liability. I did it again when I bought my Rolex watch! The end goal would be to produce enough passive income from your property that you no longer have to trade your valuable time for money. This is how I can expand my means.

The purpose of my example was to show you can become financially free while still enjoying your life on this beautiful earth. Whether you are leveraging good debt or owning assets that produce cash flow, apply this mind-set and strategy of acquiring an asset first that will then pay for your "shiny things" liabilities. This will put you on the fast track to financial freedom and wealth creation and allow you to live the life you desire.

## GOOD DEBT CAN INCREASE YOUR WEALTH

There is a new term in finance going around, and it is "phantom money." Phantom money is simply money that is invisible to the naked eye but can be used to make a visible return.

Let me explain:

- If I leverage debt through a refinance or home equity loan, then I am using phantom money.
  - Example of **Phantom money**: *Let's say I own a property worth 100K. The property appreciates a year later to 150k. I now have 50K in phantom money due to the appreciation of the asset.*
- If my company acquires an asset using a convertible note (debt) or borrowed funds, then I am using phantom money to increase my wealth.
  - Example of **Phantom money:** *Let's say I take out a SBA loan or receive financing for my business. I then use the funds to acquire assets like land, real estate, or other*

> companies using the debt loan received. The value, after these acquisitions, increases the 'good will' or intrinsic value of the business by 7x revenue. I can now sell the company for more then it cost to acquire it. This perceived value is also known as phantom money.

- If I can save money through tax exemption and avoidance, then I am creating phantom money. If you want to become wealthy, especially from nothing, then using debt the right way can make you rich.

Instead of having your child take on debt through student loans, buying an expensive car, or purchasing items with your credit card, buying cash-flowing properties through an LLC and leveraging the asset to acquire more assets can create an even greater return for you. It can also give you the cash (via good debt) you need to purchase everything else. Listen, people, we are in a debt-based monetary system, and this system is not changing anytime soon, so trying to save to pay down bad debt will leave you in a never-ending rat race. Since debt is tax-free and dollars are taxed, which makes more sense to learn to use? Instead of chasing your tail trying only to pay down debt, increase your wealth by investing in good debt— debt that other people pay, debt that is tax-free, and debt that can increase your net worth and income.

## WHY USE DEBT?

Ever since the Federal reserve's printing press began in 1971, the dollar has lost more than 90 percent of its purchasing power. The US dollar will continue to lose value due to the effects of the big bank bailouts, current wars, keeping interest rates low for a vast amount of time, and quantitative easing. Every dollar in existence is owed back with interest, so the more we print, the higher our taxes are, and the more expensive assets become due to inflation from currency printing. Now you see why it makes more sense to learn how to use debt to acquire assets that provide cash flow. This is why financial education is now more important than ever before. Instead of spending your entire life saving and working for money, you can leverage good debt to increase your wealth financially. People take on debt to seek education and buy liabilities, but very few people believe in the principle of using debt to buy assets. This is why becoming financially educated can give you a competitive edge in the inevitable shift to globalization.

**Question:** Isn't using debt to buy assets risky?

**Answer:** Not as risky as using your credit card (debt) to buy liabilities, like a pair of $500 Louis Vuitton shoes, groceries, or even your bills. The game that we are all in is about "who owes who," so if you are leveraging debt to acquire assets that someone else is paying for and what is left over is profit for you, then you are ahead of the game!

## JACK OF ALL TRADES

If you have ever heard people tell you that in order to gain wealth, you should only have one hustle, either they aren't rich or they don't want you to be. In fact, the wealthiest people in the world have multiple streams of income, not just one. You can, in fact, work for an employer or your own business, but this alone will not make you rich. If you want to acquire enough wealth to last you generations, then you need to have multiple streams of income coming in from every different category of income. These three types are the following:

1. **Ordinary**—salary or wage. Taxed 35 percent or higher
2. **Portfolio**—investments (stocks, bonds, capital gains). Taxed 15–20 percent
3. **Passive**—cash flow (dividends, cash flow). Taxed up to 15 percent

You are probably saying that this strategy can make someone "a jack of all trades but a master of none," but in doing this, you are becoming a master. You are becoming a master of cash flow and financial freedom. It does not matter if you aren't an expert in any one field as long as you can hire people who are to help you maintain it. The real objective in financial mastery is to create different streams of income (cash flow) and buy more assets from the cash flow you created through your current assets. Then use the cash flow from these assets to pay for your liabilities. In sum, if you take on massive debt, make sure someone else is paying for it.

## QUESTIONS AND ANSWERS
### Q: Can I have it all?

A: This answer is heavily dependent upon your perspective. If you approach situations as a "both, and" and learn to create "win-win" scenarios for you and others, then yes, you can have it all!

### Q: What if our monetary system changes? Should I still expand my means?

A: It does not matter what new form of money we decide to use; as long as humans continue to need human things to survive, you will have the ability to acquire more of it. So yes, the same rules of expanding your means will apply.

# Financial Freedom: *My Only Hope*

## Q: Should I expand my means in my name?

A: I strongly suggest that if you're going to adopt this principle, you set up or create an LLC that buys your income properties (good debt) from you. You want to own as little debt as possible, and if you do have debt, to make sure someone else is paying it for you.

## Q: How long will this process take?

A: Instead of asking this, I want you to ask yourself how much cash flow you will need to become financially free and comfortable. Only then will you know how long this process will take. You can always speed up the process by sacrificing your immediate pleasures (buying a luxury car, house, jewelry) for long-term wealth.

## Q: Can I expand my means in other areas of my life?

A: Sure you can! You can expand many things outside of your wealth, including your network, friendships and relationships, love, knowledge, and skill sets.

Can you come up with other ways to expand your means?
Write them down here:

1. _____

2. _____

3. _____

4. _____

5. _____

## DO YOU HAVE A LUMP SUM OF CASH?

In reality, you can in fact have it all. The goal is to have the cash flow from your assets pay for your liabilities. If you ever receive a lump sum of cash or a bonus, it is not wise to go and immediately spend it buying "toys" like cars, jewelry, bags, or clothes. This lump sum should be spent buying an asset that provides the cash flow instead. You can then utilize the cash flow from your assets to buy your "shiny" things. This is a strategy commonly used by the rich. The rich use the cash flow from their investments or leverage debt that someone else is paying for (other people's money) in order to fund their lifestyle.

# Financial Freedom: *My Only Hope*

It's very rare that the rich use their own cash to buy their "toys." This is a wasted opportunity to them. Money is capital, which means that its true goal is to make more of itself. Using your personal cash in order to buy expensive items sets you back in your pursuit to financial freedom. You can spend your money; however, you should spend it first on an asset that someone else is paying for, and then you can take your money out of that asset and use it to buy your "shiny things." This is how you become financially free and have fun along the way.

# 5

## Protect Your Assets like the Rich

What good is making a ton of money if you aren't keeping any of it? I am pretty sure that we all have heard the old saying, "It is not how much you make; it is how much you keep." This has been a common focus of the wealthy as they pursue and maintain their wealth. Asset protection along with wealth preservation has long been a focal point of the rich as they produce income or even if their businesses go insolvent. You will learn how the wealthy can protect their wealth and assets using corporations and filing for bankruptcy. You will also learn how they can hide their money in secrecy from you and the masses by not flashing or showing their wealth off. Increase your financial intelligence and understand exactly how the rich can do it all by reading the sections below.

## USE CORPORATIONS LIKE THE RICH DO

1. **Asset protection**: I do not own anything in my name, just as the rich do not. My assets are held in my C corporations, LLC, and trust. If I stumble into a lawsuit from someone looking to make a quick buck, I will not have anything to give personally.

2. **Tax and income protection**: Due to a law passed in 1943 (Current Tax Payment Act), if you are an employee of a company, the money you earn from your paycheck is immediately taxed. Have you ever noticed how your stated salary is different than what you take home every year? For example, your salary says $50,000, but you take home $26,500 after taxes. Well, that is due to this act, which was passed before you and I were even thought of. Through the Current Tax Payment Act, you are taxed the entire amount of your salary, as opposed to being taxed on what is left over after you pay to live. What makes this immediate taxation worse is that you have to live off of the $26,500, not the $50,000. You earn, then you're taxed, and then you can spend what is left over—in that order.

If you pass your income through your corporation, then you can expense your earnings before the government taxes it. It looks like this: you earn, you spend, and then the government gets to tax what is left over, if there is anything left over at all after your write-offs. (For example, I earn $50,000 through my corporation, I expense or spend $46,000 of that $50,000, and I am taxed *only* on the remaining $4,000, not the $50,000, which I would have been taxed on if I worked for a paycheck.)

## FILE FOR BANKRUPTCY LIKE THE RICH DO

Bankruptcy is another method of protection for personal assets. Bankruptcy is a legal tool used by both individuals and businesses to get rid of debt that will likely go unpaid. In a way, bankruptcy allows for a clean financial slate. With this tool, wealthy people such as 50 Cent, Donald Trump, and Henry Ford can overleverage debt, file, and come away with more money than they started with. However, personal bankruptcy and business bankruptcy are not the same things and have different rules and chapters.

## PERSONAL BANKRUPTCY—CHAPTER 7 VERSUS 13

- Chapter 7 bankruptcy is for individuals who have no hope of repaying acquired debt. This chapter is for people who have little income, and the result is a bankruptcy discharge of qualifying debt.

- Chapter 13 bankruptcy is for individuals who have income and could manage their debt if they had a payment plan. The purpose of this section is to help those who may have an improved financial condition as a result of bankruptcy or are struggling to pay debts but are not entirely destitute.

## CORPORATE/BUSINESS BANKRUPTCY—CHAPTER 7 AND 11

- Businesses may also file under Chapter 7, but the result is the dissolution of the entity instead of reorganization.
- Chapter 11 bankruptcy is for businesses, including corporations, to either reorganize or liquidate their assets to repay debt. Most of the time, a Chapter 11 filing results in a reorganization. Debtors get to propose their plans at first, but after a certain amount of time has passed, creditors may also submit restructuring plans. The creditors have to vote to approve whatever plan is selected.

Individuals can file under Chapter 11, but since this section is more complicated, most people opt for a Chapter 7 or 13 bankruptcy.

## GENERAL DIFFERENCES BETWEEN BUSINESS AND PERSONAL BANKRUPTCY

One of the significant differences between personal and business bankruptcy is the means test. Individuals have to participate in one to determine if they are eligible for a Chapter 7 or a Chapter 13, while businesses do not have to prove this for a Chapter 11 filing. Businesses can also cancel contracts with creditors if it would be financially favorable to both parties to do so, while individuals do not get that option for student loan debt or other types of debt exempt from bankruptcy.

This is another way the wealthy are protected. Due to lack of knowledge and financial literacy, the poor and middle class saddled with personal debt are forced to accept penalties associated with filing for personal bankruptcy, such as negative remarks on credit reports and still being on the hook to pay student loans (if they have any).

## THE ULTRARICH DON'T FLASH

Do you ever see Bill Gates wearing a $100,000 chain, Dr. Dre showing off the cash he made from the sale of Beats by Dre, or even Elon Musk flaunting himself in any of the rockets he owns? If the answer is no, then why are you showing your stuff off? Buying to keep up with the Kardashians not only sets you back financially but also makes you a target. Now, I am not saying you shouldn't experience luxury. What I am saying is if you are going to buy something expensive, make sure you are buying it for yourself and it's not going to put a huge dent in your finances. You know who you are. And you know what I am referring to. I understand that the media, advertisement companies, and public perception make this task of delayed gratification a difficult one to accomplish, but in doing this you will set yourself free mentally and financially. Think about how much of your money has been quietly siphoned back to the rich by your uncontrollable consumption of high-end items like Gucci, Louis Vuitton, Birkin bags, and Mercedes Benz. Now ask yourself, "Is my appetite to spend money to flaunt driven by the media or public perception, or is it really due to low self-esteem?"

Instead, imagine how much cash flow you would have if you only waited on buying these items and purchased assets first. I guarantee that if you apply this philosophy to your life and start buying assets first, you will begin to understand that you don't need to flash when you really have it. You will see that if you want it, you can get it and still be financially strong. I bet my life that the more you begin to understand how money works and how to create money from money, you will skip on buying that Bentley and buy the island instead. Or if you do buy the Bentley, you will go out your way to make sure that you use none of your cash to purchase it.

## WHY DELAWARE?

Since the inception of the American establishment, Delaware has been the primary hub for all corporations and entities looking to exist in a tax- and law-friendly state. Delaware is home to more than half of all public and Fortune 500 companies. These companies include Apple, Coca-Cola, DuPont, Sallie Mae, and many more. There are three main benefits for people who want to incorporate their company there:

- An established and business-friendly legal structure
- A widely respected and experienced court system
- Pro-business regulations from the state government

Have you ever heard of Zynga? Well, Zynga was one of the 86 percent of all the new IPOs incorporated in Delaware. Even big tech companies like Google are beginning to see the benefit in having a C corporation in Delaware. I know firsthand that even incubators such as Y Combinator look for new start-ups that are incorporated in Delaware, as it allows an organization to issue shares without a hiccup. Speaking to the *New York Times*, David Brunori, a George Washington University Law School professor and tax expert, explained that "Delaware is an outlier in the way it does business...What it offers is an opportunity to game the system and do it legally."

Now that is my type of state! With all of the new innovative companies still looking to this state as a place of incorporation, along with tax experts singing its praises, you can see why Delaware is considered the "corporate capital of the world," right?

## WHAT HAPPENS IN VEGAS

I now have a new reason to head to Vegas for the weekend—Nevada! This place is another tax haven for corporations. As a starting point, for most of you who have an international holdings company or technology company earning licensing, copyright, or patenting fees, it is appropriate to set up a business in Nevada. This is simply because, from a tax point of view, you do not pay business income tax from this state if you, as the owner of the business, do not live or operate in this state (the same applies in Delaware). Another significant benefit is that holding companies, typically set up in the state of Nevada, can hold companies in various states.

For example, let's say that I own five McDonald's franchises all operating in five different states, and I set up a holdings corporation called Jay Enterprises. My holdings company, which is registered in Nevada, can own these five subsidiary companies (the five McDonald's franchises) registered in these different states. This is considered an advanced strategy, but I advise you reach out to your CPA or an attorney to see how to handle your particular situation.

## JUST A BIT OF CAUTION

If you have a brick-and-mortar business or own a franchise or a small business, then operating within your state will suffice. The above options are mainly for technology companies or umbrella corporations that own multiple businesses. This is because it may cost you much more financially and legally to operate a traditional brick-and-mortar business outside of the state your business is physically located in. There is little to no flexibility unless you have multiple companies outside of one area and you need to allocate the revenue into a corporation. Only then should you register with Delaware and Nevada. Also, the states want to know who the resident is to serve papers, legal documents, and notices to. So if you decide to incorporate and don't live in these states, you will need to pay a company (or someone) a monthly fee to act as a registered agent to satisfy the state's requirement of having someone local to send the information to.

In my opinion, it's very imprudent not to incorporate your business. However, you should only have a certain level of business for it to be beneficial for you. For example, if you are only generating $10K–30K a year in revenue, then it may *not* make sense to incorporate. But once your business reaches a certain level, you will have to do so to protect your assets and to validate your company.

With this information, I have provided you with the best way to incorporate by setting up your entities in these tax-haven states. Having your corporation set up in Nevada or Delaware can be a great strategy if you are seeking the necessary protection and flexible regulations. The rest is up to you. Make sure you are consulting with your attorney or tax advisor if you would like to take the step to incorporate. Learning to understand and adopt these legal principles that the wealthy use can enable you to not only increase your wealth but also preserve and protect it. We have been taught that these strategies are immoral, difficult to achieve, and even volatile. However, the rich can take on risk and win at the game simply because they protect themselves using the strategies mentioned in the text. I advise that you learn this aspect of the game, as it will be your shield and protection from the hardships of business. There is no need to be afraid to get into the game, because like in many games, there are do-overs and cheat codes that give you the advantage you need to win. Most importantly, good luck and get started!

## LEGACY, LEGACY, LEGACY

Generational wealth—that is the key! The Rockefeller name is synonymous with the term "legacy" for the family's ability to pass its wealth down through generations over a century! John D. Rockefeller's primary mandate after acquiring his fortune in the early 1900s was to preserve it and pass it down from one generation to the next. In 1934, John D. Rockefeller Jr. established trusts for his daughter and five sons that consisted of oil company stocks and real estate holdings. As a result, the Rockefeller family still maintains their fortune today. We have now witnessed an awakening of wealth preservation and ownership transfer extending from the Walton family (Walmart) all the way to the Carter family (Jay-Z and Beyoncé).

The basic and most common types of trust funds you often hear about are revocable and irrevocable trusts.

Revocable trust just means you, as a grantor, can modify the trust at any point in time. Irrevocable trust means that you are waiving your right to ownership of any assets held in the trust. So think carefully about who you decide to place under this kind of trust!

No matter how minuscule your wealth may appear, you must ensure that you are creating a legacy. Whether you plan to will your money to your kids or to someone you love, you must learn how the wealthy can pass down their wealth by using tools such as trust funds and estate planning. The wealthy have long been able to keep their money, even after death, through applying practical methods like the ones mentioned. Anyone can create a family dynasty and legacy. However, doing this requires a burning desire to end a perpetual cycle of poverty within your family. It also requires you to build and preserve your money and become selfless. If these families can do it, so can you. Now it's your turn to start!

# 6

# Failure Is the Best Degree

Have you failed in life? Well, congratulations; here is your diploma. With this award, you've earned your master's in wisdom.

I have to admit I wouldn't have been able to acquire this level of knowledge without my own shortcomings. I remember losing my first $15,000 speculating in the stock market. Unfortunately, I was on the wrong side of the oil slide. I was jobless, with only $15,000, and a $1,200 rent hovering over my head. Those who have been in a similar situation of having cash with no income know the intrinsic stress that comes with being unemployed with dwindling cash. Subsequently, after about one hundred employment rejection e-mails, I decided to take control of my life by investing in the stock market.

# Financial Freedom: *My Only Hope*

*You cannot have a testimony without the test.*

*- Nina Turner*

## DUMB LUCK AND EGO

**"Failing is how you learn in the real world.
In the real world, you fail until you succeed"**

*— Rich Dad, Poor Dad.*

I still remember my first trade. The stock was LinkedIn, and the company was in the midst of releasing its quarterly earnings report, which would give the stock a significant swing (up or down) in price. After conducting research, I found that LinkedIn had never yet had a negative earnings report. So I did what financial pundits would consider financial suicide and bought $15,000 (all of my money) worth of shares. Listen, the only other time I have ever experienced that level of anxiety was when I got pulled over by a police officer at three in the morning in an alleyway. The only influence propelling me forward in this situation was desperation and the fear of going broke. I purchased the shares two hours before the close so that I could capitalize on the momentum of other idio…I mean traders looking to do the same thing that I was. Once I heard the chimes of the closing bell, I knew that it was too late to turn back. Now all that was left was a waiting game to hear the results. I watched apprehensively as the CNBC reporters announced the negative earnings report of other companies releasing their earnings that day. I just knew it was over. Then I heard one of the reporters say, "Just in. We've attained LinkedIn's quarterly results." They were positive. The stock had jumped up forty-five points in one day! I made $3,200 in one day of trading, bringing my total principal to about $18,200. It was an exhilarating experience. I did it again the following week with Amazon and then with Facebook. In total, I made an extra $9,000 doing this. I was so successful at this that I started believing my hype. I thought I was a financial guru. I was sorely mistaken. I invested in an oil company, looking to capitalize on the short-term rebound. I lost $8,000 in twenty-four hours, and two weeks later, the company went belly up. I lost everything. This taught me a very valuable lesson in investing, and that is why I am extremely analytical when I am approaching any investment endeavor now.

## BLESSED BY FAILURE

This unfortunate occurrence was a blessing in disguise. It taught me to analyze a company's books, financials, and industry trends before deciding on purchasing its stock. I don't own a single stock that doesn't pay me a dividend. I look for cash flow—cash after capital expenditures. If the stock is not returning cash, I don't want it. I don't care if it is the next Facebook, Snapchat, Uber, or whatever. The reason is that you can't lie about cash. A company can tell the greatest story of all time, but I will only listen to its financial statements. If it were not for my risky speculation, I would not have seen the value in research, structure, and dividend-paying companies.

> *Failure is the opportunity to begin, again*
> *only this time, more wisely.*

> — HENRY FORD

If you are looking for a degree that will propel you to exponential financial education and wisdom, then failure is the right major for you (as long as you are learning from it). I don't look at failure like our school system does. If you fail in school, it's like you are the worst person in the world and you're going to die a thousand deaths tomorrow and rot in hell. But that is not necessarily the case when it comes to reaching financial freedom. In this quest and game, you have to learn through trial and error to understand it. That is why more than 80 percent of second-generation heirs who inherit money lose it. It's not money that makes you wealthy; it's knowledge.

## FAIL FAST

*I have not failed. I've just found ten thousand ways that won't work.*

—THOMAS EDISON

Do any of your fears consist of the following?

- Fear of failure
- Fear of rejection
- Fear of looking stupid
- Fear of messing up
- Fear of being wrong publicly
- Fear of being exposed

The longer it takes for you to embrace and get over your failures, the longer it will take for you to learn from them. I recommend that if you must fail, you should fail fast and learn from your failures even more quickly. Some failures may require more time to come back from than others, and others may even leave a bad taste in your mouth as you try to move forward from them. However, to move forward from these mishaps, I want you to ask yourself, "Did I die, or did I kill someone else?" If you did, then God bless you; I have nothing for you. However, if you didn't, lighten up! What didn't kill you (or anyone else) will only make you stronger and wiser. Embrace failure, because this is your inner compass; your inner divinity is checking in and putting you back on course to receive your true blessing. This is a blessing that no human engineering can ever take from you. This blessing is divine, and embracing failure is the key to unlocking this divinity. So don't be afraid of failure so much that you aren't willing to try and reach your true greatness. Understand that there is no security in life, only opportunity. Embrace it, learn from it, and move on! Because if you aren't moving, you might as well be dead.

## SCHOOL: DON'T ASK FOR HELP ON THE TEST

I can attest; I wasn't the smartest person in the classroom, nor was I even an A student. I was an average student at best in the eyes of our education system. In fact, there were a few occasions when I got in serious trouble for asking someone for help during a test or while writing my term paper. I never understood during my time in school why students were forced to work individually on extensive assignments and tests and would be punished for asking for help from their classmates. In the real world, asking for help can be the difference between failure and success. In the real world, if I am engaging in a business deal and I am handed a term sheet, I am reaching out to my attorney for help. If I am looking for a cash-flowing property in a desirable area, I am reaching out to some of my friends who are experts in real estate. If I want to learn how to lose weight, I am getting help from a personal trainer. However, if I am asking my friends for help on the test, I automatically get a failing grade. Why is that?

- Shouldn't schools be more focused on human collaboration as opposed to separating people based on test scores?
- Have schools and universities reinforced the notion of social Darwinism by manufacturing their form of survival of the fittest?
- Are individual tests in schools the solution to economic growth and prosperity for all?

- Are schools implemented to either discriminate against people who excel in spaces outside of indoctrination or prepare students only for the workforce?

I believe some of my past failures were due to feeling like I had all the right answers. By feeling like this, I did not allow myself to work with anyone or ask for help. I believe we all experience this feeling of grandiosity and belief that we are above our peers. We think that because we excel in the education system, corporate environment, or other systems, that we are too sophisticated to ask for help, or we are too embarrassed to do so. We parade around our indoctrinated education, all while being saddled with debt and working for a person who flunked out of the system we excelled in. Do you see the problem here?

*The real work begins after you graduate.*

— SYDNEY ALSTON

Why do we have to go to school? My guess is so that we can be trained to repeat information and think like the status quo instead of learning how to think freely and independently. Once we graduate, we will get a job and work to survive, pay taxes to fund our political aristocrats, and perpetuate the corporate system of indentured servitude.

## I'M NEVER GOING TO HAVE ENOUGH MONEY TO DO WHAT I WANT TO DO

The truth is, no matter how wealthy you are, you will never have enough money to do everything that you desire to do in life. The human mind is very expansive and riddled with so many unique and valid ideas, and these ideas are infinite. Instead of focusing on how much money you have or trying not to lose it, I challenge you to think differently. Ask yourself, "How many lives am I affecting, and what value am I creating and offering in the world?" I guarantee that if you focus on affecting millions of lives, then you will see how much money that is worth. As the saying goes, "To get a billion dollars, you must change billions of lives." Having such a mind-set separates the millionaires from the billionaires. Try to create a product or innovation that will make billions of lives easier, and if you fail, try to build something else that will do it. Remember, it only takes one successful idea or product to change your entire trajectory. So keep on failing. Fail until you succeed!

## EDUCATION IS A LIFETIME PROCESS THAT LASTS A LIFETIME

> *If you think education is expensive, wait until you see how much ignorance costs in the twenty-first century.*

—FORMER PRESIDENT OBAMA

I am never not learning. There are so many things that I am still searching for in life. With the infinite deviations of knowledge, along with so many different learning experiences, chances are that I may never reach a point of knowing everything. This is why universal education and financial literacy are so important. Sure, we see the inflated cost of acquiring knowledge, from the increasing prices of TED talks and seminars to real estate courses and formal education. However, I'd rather pay the cost of learning and doing than pay for the inevitable result of ignorance.

Education enables us to stay humble, poised, and, most importantly, present in life. The ability to further educate ourselves will continue to accelerate our intelligence and spark our inner curiosity, or, in other words, our inner child. When you trigger your inner child, you can imagine and create things unimaginable to an indoctrinated and tainted mind. Tapping into this subconscious mind through education is not only beneficial to you but also to the world around you. Curiosity breeds innovation, and innovation is the essence of growth within humanity. You have a genius that is needed in this world, but to unlock your genius, you need the key to education—in any form. Once you start to educate yourself, you will soon discover the abundant and endless number of opportunities that exist in and around your world. You will see your world open up and get a better understanding of your purpose in it. We all have an important role in this world, so let's educate ourselves in every capacity and learn from real-world simulation and application. Only then will we begin to open our minds and see the world as a place of opportunity and endless possibilities.

## UNLOCK YOUR INNER CHILD

*Two most important days are the day you're born and the day that you find out why.*

*- Mark Twain.*

# Financial Freedom: *My Only Hope*

This segment is geared toward my over analytical folks, the people who suffer from a pervasive disorder known as "analysis paralysis." You know exactly who you are. Please understand this: the difference between a successful person and everyone else is simple—execution. After analyzing all of the data and variables known to man, my advice to you is short and sweet. To relinquish analysis paralysis, unlock your inner child and "just do it" already, only if you feel good about the opportunity. If you were a child and you wanted to go to Disneyland, I am pretty sure that you wouldn't second-guess yourself or weigh the pros and cons. This sense of innocence apparently leaves us when we are tainted by society as we get older. I believe that tapping into your inner child sparks the essence of creativity and opportunity and allows you to ignore your ignorance. It enables you to pursue anything that you can imagine without fearing the consequences of failure or the "what if" scenario. I assure you that once you apply the "inner child" mentality after evaluating an opportunity, you will be able to make a decision with equanimity and see it through unapologetically.

## TAPPING INTO YOUR SUBCONSCIOUS MIND

Tapping into your subconscious mind extends far beyond the fabric of our external thoughts. Your conscious mind is only the tiniest step of a vast pyramid of knowledge hiding within you. It is in this subconscious that you contain a great amount of knowledge, memories, and wisdom that you are probably critically underutilizing. Learning to unlock your subconscious mind can unleash your true potential and radically transform your life. The interesting thing about your subconscious mind is that it cannot tell the difference between reality and your imagination. In other words, if you can visualize it, then it can happen!

## HOW CAN I TAP INTO MY SUBCONSCIOUS MIND?

The answer relies on three simple but powerful steps:

1. First, the key is to firmly believe that you are already in possession of that which you desire. This is a **Be-Do-Have** exercise. To have, you have to become it, then do the work to make it a reality. If you want to be rich, you have to think like a rich person, and as a result, you will start to do what rich people do and obtain what rich people have.

2. Second, you must have such an intense **belief in yourself** and what you want to acquire that your subconscious starts to accept it and begins to act on it. This is the equivalent of telling yourself that you're the greatest well before the world does.

3.  The final step that aids in your ability to tap into your subconscious mind comes in the form of **affirmations**. Whether you desire wealth, love, comfort, success, happiness, or financial freedom, repeating affirmations daily can train your mind to act on them even when you aren't thinking about your affirmations.

By following these three steps religiously, you will begin to see that impossibility is frivolous! You will also notice that your circumstances will not define your destination. We all have the power to change our financial situations and reach financial freedom. However, you have to believe in yourself so much that you see failure not as a roadblock but as lanes guiding you to your true destination. Failure is God's way of putting you right back on track to receive your blessing. These blessings can come in many forms. In my opinion, the blessing can rest within your subconscious mind and formulate itself as a strong belief in oneself. Start to set your mind free and believe in your capabilities to achieve financial freedom or any other goal that you may have, because freeing yourself from any doubts, failures, or considerations is the key to tapping into your subconscious mind.

# 7

# You Are Not an Island

Have you ever heard the statement "The whole is greater than the sum of its parts"? This phrase is extremely valid and will help you understand how to build a multinational company. The Great Wall of China, Egypt, the Roman Empire, and the United States of America were not made by one man. These diverse accomplishments were constructed by a team of like-minded people. There were systems established because the vision was bigger than the individual. To build a system like that, you have to make the team understand that your idea, business, and vision are bigger than you are! There has to be a sense of selflessness and leadership that forces you to relinquish your control and be a part of a team. As the saying goes, there is no "I" in the word "team."

## IT'S OKAY; RELINQUISH CONTROL

I know you want that title all to yourself. I believe you know what title I am referring to: Chief Executive Officer (CEO). There is nothing more gratifying in business than having those particular four words on your business cards: "I am CEO, bitch!" But is this all that you want? Would you rather have a title than an actual business? Inevitably, people who start their own companies automatically appoint themselves as the CEOs. However, though there are different ways to be a chief executive officer of a company, many of us resort to only one method of command, and that is the famous "do it yourself" (DIY) model. Are there some cases where this model works? Sure, if you are self-employed and offer a particular skill set, such as being a doctor or lawyer. But if you're trying to build a big business, the DIY method poses a few problems.

1. The company can't move quickly
2. Ideas are often limited, due to having only one mind
3. You don't know everything
4. It is exhausting

Being able to relinquish control is pivotal to the growth and success of your business or project. If you want your company to move quickly and adapt to the rapid changes and innovations that occur, then having a team mentality is the right way to go. Having this mind-set will allow you to focus on the big picture while you have your team take care of the small tasks that are required to execute the big picture. In my case, having my team handle the little things allows me to think more clearly and focus on the overall vision of my company. My business can move quickly, and all of the simple tasks like getting incorporated, filing taxes, and doing other paperwork are taken care of. Now, when I say "team," I am referring to my accountant, lawyer, and business advisor. These are the people who make sure the glue sticks to the parts that I am assembling. In other words, they take care of the tedious work that would have otherwise taken up more of my time to complete. A team can be anything. It can be your mother doing your laundry for you while you study for a big exam, your wife helping you become a better man, or even your grandmother signing onto your loan as a guarantor for you to continue to invest in cash flow properties. A good team helps ease the pain of accomplishing a goal and helps speed up the process. Do teams fuck up? Sure they do! Are they human? Sure they are. Humans require a lot of care, forgiveness, and positive reinforcement to keep producing for you. If you are impatient or a control freak, you will look at having a team as a negative. I see it differently. My team members are my allies.

## YOU GET BETTER RESULTS BY SYNERGIZING

Simply put, synergizing is about the notion of more heads being better than one. Let's say that I am running a security company providing top-notch security for high-profile athletes. There is another person named Jessica who has a security company that is focused on musicians, and there is another person named John who owns a similar security firm but provides the equipment and cargo for all the other security companies. These three security companies, including myself, are all fighting for the same contracts. What I would do is say, "Why don't we synergize, leverage all of our resources, reduce our overhead cost, and become the preeminent security firm in the United States?" Through the power of synergizing, the proficiency of invention and innovation will increase exponentially.

## ONE HUNDRED PERCENT OF NOTHING IS JUST THAT

There is nothing more detrimental to the success of a business than having no cash flow, team, or working capital. I have been there before, refusing to bring on investors and turning down deals simply because I didn't want to give away equity. But the truth is that to grow, you have to give a little. Now, I am not saying that you should abandon the farm and sell your entire stake in your company for capital, I am only saying that it is wise to know that 100 percent of nothing is just that.

I initially struggled to get my business to scale because I did not want to offer any equity to a potential growth hacker. I had little to no revenue coming in and lacked a sufficiently talented programmer on my team. It was not until I searched through my network via LinkedIn that I came across exactly what I needed. He was a growth hacker who worked with many of the top tech companies in the industry, such as Snapchat, Skurt, and The Honest Company. While viewing his resume, I found that he played a pivotal part in helping these companies reach massive scale and growth within their user bases. I immediately reached out to ask him to join our team. After hearing my pitch, he became interested in moving forward in joining. There was one issue, however. He wanted a ton of equity. He asked for 12 percent of the company! I immediately turned down the offer, forgetting about providing a cliff as a trial period before releasing the 12 percent equity to him. I later regretted my decision. Looking back now, I realized that letting go of 12 percent equity would have gotten me over ten thousand users in less than a month. I left a ton of money on the table doing this.

# Financial Freedom: *My Only Hope*

I witness so many entrepreneurs fall into this growth trap all the time. They are never open to the opportunity cost of trading equity for talent or money and fall into the abyss because of this choice. I'd say if you have something smart or valuable enough to get the attention of someone willing to invest, but they want a substantial amount of equity for money, consider it and close the deal! I can't recall how many times I've watched the television show *Shark Tank* only to see entrepreneurs with no revenue or proven track record turn away money because the equity stake was too high. Unless you have an outrageous amount of revenue or users, take the deal! You have the power to produce an infinite amount of value through many of your ideas, Trust me.

Mark Zuckerberg owned only 17 percent of his company by the time it reached a billion-dollar valuation. Dr. Dre held a third of his own business, and Elon Musk sold many of his billion-dollar companies. Musk went from selling his first software company to founding PayPal, selling his stake in PayPal, and founding Tesla Motors and SpaceX.

I am not pointing to the skill of building sophisticated companies but to the understanding of how to leverage an exit to produce more streams of income. These examples show how you go from 100 percent of nothing to 20 percent of a billion-dollar empire.

## CREATE A SYSTEM—PEOPLE, PROCESS, AND PRODUCT

Marcus Lemonis has been credited as the pioneer of this concept. During his television show, *The Profit*, he shares his knowledge of how to create a system that will allow your business to exist and function outside of you. Marcus explains how the three Ps (people, process, and product) are the engine that makes the car go. Without these three systems in place, it is often very challenging to get a start-up off of the ground, let alone raise capital. A leader is a critical component to the implementation of the three Ps system. Not having a clear leader is a big problem in any business. A lack of leadership provides a lack of clarity. A lack of transparency provides a lack of efficiency. And as efficiency drops, so do the two Ms: margins and morale in the workplace. All of that equates to bad margins and less business. So, to grow any entrepreneurial endeavor, focus on the three Ps of business development—people (a stable and reliable team), process (an efficient and streamlined system), and lastly, product (a dynamic and differentiated business or model).

## CAPITALISM VERSUS MANAGERIAL CAPITALISM

Congratulations on getting that high-paying job at Goldman Sachs, KPMG, or any other large corporation! You are now a managerial capitalist. You control other people's money and budget, and you have borrowed power and influence. This is not a jab or insult; I am only pointing to the fact that there is a difference between you (a managerial capitalist) and an entrepreneur (an actual capitalist). Sure, you can sit on top of your $150,000-plus salary and frown upon or even laugh at a broke and struggling entrepreneur, but I assure you that his or her value in our economy is just as important as yours.

Sadly, most people today do not understand the difference between being a true capitalist and being a managerial capitalist. C-suite executives and CEOs are often seen by the media as the modern-day capitalists of our society. However, I believe this is far from the truth. Many of these people are takers, selfish, and often greedy. This is shown through CEOs being paid huge bonuses while cutting thousands of jobs within their workforce. This is also exhibited through stock buyback. Stock buyback is when a CEO borrows money from the banks (usually during lower interest rates) and uses the funds to buy back company stock to increase the stock price. Instead of creating more jobs or investing in R&D that will help the business grow, the CEOs increase the stock price, allowing them to grow their wealth. Is this the result of the knowledge taught in business schools and MBA programs? Are they teaching our students the nature of greed and the "profit over anything" mentality? Or are they teaching them how to build sustainable companies, become givers, and create value for others?

Here is a quote Dr. Frank Luntz's book, *What Americans Really Want...Really*:

"So how to equip a generation of Americans for success in entrepreneurship? Forget about MBA's. Most business schools teach you how to be successful in big corporations rather than start your own company. But starting something from scratch and maturing it as it grows is where our country has been at its strongest and most innovative."

True capitalists, in my opinion, are givers. They are the people who display the ability to empathize with the masses and create value for not only themselves but for others. Entrepreneurs like Sean Carter, Sean Combs, Steve Jobs, Elon Musk, Jimmy Iovine, Bill Gates, Jack Dorsey, and Jessica Alba have all created value and put in the legwork to build large companies from conception. These real capitalists did not need to attend an MBA program to become successful. In fact, the best education one can receive is real-world simulation and experience. This type of education is priceless, comes with failure, and requires a ton of selflessness and empathy. Rather than knowing how to spend money like a managerial capitalist, real capitalists know how to create and make money from nothing. They are the reasons corporations are established in the first place and why managerial capitalists even have jobs. Without real capitalism and entrepreneurship, there would be no jobs, innovation, or productivity within our society.

Entrepreneurs, our true capitalists, are the pillars of civilization, and we need more of these kinds of capitalists in our communities. These types of people put up their own money, take huge risks, spearhead innovation, and create jobs for others. They are the givers of modern society, and we should appreciate and applaud them, no matter their economic position in our community.

## I AM MARRIED TO AN ENTREPRENEUR; NOW WHAT?

Before I begin, let me first pray for you. This is going to be a journey unlike anything you've ever experienced in your life. Should be fun, right? I wish the answer to this question were that easy. Okay, let me sum this up for you. Get ready to endure some of the toughest times in your life! Unless your significant other inherited wealth or won money, this experience will not only challenge your mental and spiritual needs, it will also challenge your relationship. However, once you guys finally accomplish this goal of self-dependence, your bond will grow stronger, financial abundance will materialize, and you guys will be prepared for anything that comes your way. Remember this: tough times don't last, but tough people do.

Being an entrepreneur, let alone being married to one, is like playing with fire or running near the edge of a cliff. It is incredibly dangerous. I often refer to my fellow entrepreneurs as the "bad boys" of society. They march to the beat of their own drums and resist being part of the status quo. This challenge or disruption, does not come without its drawbacks. Since entrepreneurs are the outliers of the working class, they are often ostracized and made to fend for themselves to survive. It's the equivalent of being cast out of society. Knowing this is one thing, but understanding entrepreneurs' mind-sets and existing in their world is like decoding an Egyptian scroll—exhausting, challenging, and overwhelming. To combat this, two things must take place. You either have to throw in the towel at whatever point the entrepreneur is at, or ride the roller coaster of uncertainty until the person succeeds and support them through the ups and downs.

Understand that there is a light at the end of the tunnel. If and when your significant other reaches maximum success, you will reap the benefits of exponential abundance. What that abundance is depends on your situation or relationship. But I know for certain that your trust, belief, and loyalty will propel you to first place on that rewards list. Beyond material rewards, just the satisfaction and happiness that come with witnessing and being part of someone's journey to success can be just as intoxicating. In the end, you will never lose as long as you understand why you are loyal and that you care about someone winning more than the benefits you may reap in the end. So try to remain supportive and stick it out, as long as you are not being drained physically, spiritually, mentally, and emotionally in the process.

## I AM MARRIED TO SOMEONE WHO ISN'T AN ENTREPRENEUR; NOW WHAT?

I am going to play devil's advocate here. Do you not understand that you are in a partnership? You do know that your partner is his or her individual with his or her own goals, ambitions, and passions, right? Sure, your entrepreneurial endeavor may work, but what if you're wrong and the market doesn't want what you have to offer? Have you considered what you are going to do in the meantime to support your partner, or more importantly, yourself? These are some of the questions you have to ask yourself before embarking on any journey while being in a relationship, let alone an entrepreneurial journey.

Having an entrepreneur's mentality while being in a relationship with someone who has an employee and stability mentality can be quite daunting. I've witnessed so many relationships end because of the drastic differences in financial ideology and bank accounts. One person values the safety and security of a check, while the other appreciates the thought of financial freedom and the free enterprise system (starting a business). These differences tend to create resentment and anger in couples. It is unfortunate that society measures masculinity based on the number of dollars a person has in their pockets. However, survival is a key indicator of a man's worthiness to a woman, and if he can generate money, then in her mind, they can survive.

My suggestion to anyone, man or woman, who is an entrepreneur going through what is mentioned above is that you must focus on building yourself financially and personally before deciding to get into a relationship with someone who has an employee mind-set. I say this is because as an entrepreneur, there will be times when you have to eat ramen noodles and sacrifice your lifestyle to build your business or start a new endeavor. If you are in a relationship (short or long term) with someone who cannot do this, then having open communication and transparency may buy you the time you need to stay focused on reaching your goals and building. There will be times when you may feel emasculated, incompetent, or even a burden, but if you want to be in a relationship with this person, then you have to learn how to ignore these thoughts and emotions. Only then will you have the equanimity to keep your eye on the prize and accomplish your goal of reaching financial freedom as an entrepreneur.

# 8

# How Financial Intelligence Creates Wealth

I always wondered why financial education isn't taught in our schools. I guess the system probably doesn't want the masses to be that financially intelligent. If you become financially intelligent, then your dependence on the system ceases to exist. Besides, independence of the masses is powerful and dangerous to an aristocratic empire like ours. There is a reason why college is a $26 trillion industry and why some of the wealthiest people in the world dropped out of it. School prepares you only for the workforce (we can even argue the effectiveness of that), and life is about more than just working to survive. I don't know about you, but all of the knowledge that I've acquired in regard to money was based on real-world simulation, not the education system. I had to educate myself outside of school to set myself free financially. My job is to help you do the same, so I will break down financial intelligence and explain how it can help you create wealth.

## WHAT IS WEALTH?

I define wealth as the number of days you can survive without working. In my opinion, wealth is measured in time, not dollars. For example, if your expenses are $1,000 a month and you have $4,000 in savings, then your wealth is measured at exactly four months, or 120 days. Real wealth is simply our time. But we trade away moments of our time, day by day, year by year, for money, just to spend it on items that require us to work more to maintain them. These liabilities force us to trade more of our time to make up for the money lost. This repetitive cycle of trading time for money puts us in a never-ending rat race coercing us to chase something that always seems to get away from us.

**Question:** What is the prime asset of life? If you said "time," then you are likely part of the 0.01 percent of the population that doesn't waste any of it!

## FINANCIAL INTELLIGENCE

What is financial intelligence? Well, first, I will tell you what it is not. Spending your life working hard for money only to have it go out faster than it came in is not financial intelligence. In my opinion, financial intelligence can be defined in the following ways:

1. Converting cash into assets that produce cash flow
2. Looking at deals through logic and not emotion
3. Understanding the difference between assets and liabilities
4. Understanding how to increase your income by leveraging good debt

These are all signs of financial intelligence. Whenever someone asks me, "What can you tell me about financial intelligence?" my answer is always the same: "Give me a million dollars, and you'll find out." Understanding your value can also be a form of financial intelligence. All too often, our lack of financial intelligence puts us on the wrong side of the game. Yes, we are playing an economic game of who is indebted to whom. And the more people you are indebted to, the poorer you will be. If you have too much bad debt, society begins to take everything you have and produce. It takes your time, your life, your confidence, your dignity, and anything else if you let it. This game is a game of wolf versus sheep. This game is a game of takers. If you are financially uninformed and lack the proper financial education, then you will be considered sheep and become indebted to the world. My job is to help you understand the game and play it better than anyone else. If you follow my teachings, you will tap into this power and hopefully use it for good.

## CAPITAL GAINS: SELL THE EGGS, NOT THE GOOSE

Have you ever read the story of the goose that laid the golden eggs? This simple story applies to finance in so many ways. In our current economy, the people who get crushed are the people who invest for capital gains and not cash flow. It does not matter what market you are in. Whether it's stocks, commodities, real estate, or business, if you are going into it hoping to sell to a bigger idiot than you, you are playing the wrong game.

Let's look at a brief example of someone buying for capital gains:

- You buy something at $5 and hope to sell it later for $10. You purchase a house for $300,000 and hope to flip it for $600,000. You buy a penny stock for $0.05 and try to sell it for more.

These examples show people investing for capital gains. When I invest, I invest for cash flow. In my opinion, how I invest is a lot like the game Monopoly. It goes as follows:

- One green house gives me $50; two green houses give me $100. Three green houses give me $150, and then I do what is called a 1031 exchange and buy one red hotel that makes me $500 in cash flow.

It's not rocket science! You don't even need a high school diploma to understand this basic formula of wealth creation. I just keep buying assets, and they pay me a consistent monthly income. The more assets I accumulate, the more I make in monthly income. It is just that simple. Capital gains mean that hopefully there is someone stupid enough to relieve you of your stupidity. So if you're going to be smart, play the cash flow game. This will allow you to increase your wealth and get a positive income at the same time.

## WHY WOULD YOU EAT THE GOOSE?
Capital gains are like eating the goose instead of the golden eggs. It's foolish; why would you eat something that is producing

golden eggs? Why would you eat the goose? There is a reason so many people in low-income communities got wiped out during the subprime crisis in 2008. The government went into the poorest communities and played on their dreams of getting rich through real estate. The people within these communities started becoming flippers, overleveraging their debt loads and buying houses at inflated prices in hopes to sell to a bigger idiot. As the financial meltdown ensued, property values plummeted, and people in low-income areas such as Baltimore, Detroit, Cleveland, and Los Angeles lost everything. In my opinion, investing in real estate, stocks, or any other investment vehicle for capital gains is a Ponzi scheme. You are hoping that there is a bigger fool than you who will take on your financial nightmare. I don't know about you, but playing speculation causes too much stress and anxiety for me. If I am not able to predict the future, or deceive someone, then it is challenging to make profit speculating. I'd rather invest for cash flow and have the capital appreciation be the icing on the cake to my investment.

> *Buy your "toys" like clothes, cars, and vacation homes off profits of profits, and never spend the principal. Build profits, and then enjoy the cash flow you receive from them. But never, ever spend the principal.*
>
> *— KEVIN O'LEARY*

## EQ VERSUS IQ (EMOTIONAL INTELLIGENCE VERSUS INTELLECTUAL INTELLIGENCE)

Having a high IQ can, in fact, make you rich in life. You can use your gift of talent, intellect, or education to produce massive amounts of money for yourself. But emotional intelligence enables you to become wealthy. Emotional intelligence or EQ is known as the wealthy's intelligence, and it manifests as the ability to delay instant gratification. In my opinion, this is why the poor and middle class struggle. The middle class probably displays the highest IQ levels known to man, yet is still considered middle—mediocre, in my opinion. These middle-class people are the doctors, executives, or accountants who live in the only million-dollar houses they own. These people own a vacation property on the side that produces little to no cash flow for them and have a million dollars (or two) wrapped in stock, bonds, 401(k) plans, and mutual funds. This sounds great if you're selfish. But I believe in building communities and generational wealth. Although these people may appear rich, they are in fact one job or income loss away from desperation and a shot to the ego.

## FINANCIAL IQ REQUIRES 90 PERCENT EQ

Having a high EQ means displaying the ability to forgo any emotional impulse you may have to think clearly and logically.

These emotional whims that many people with high IQs face include fear, greed, envy, happiness, and other emotions. Having high emotional intelligence, however, allows you to suppress these emotions and make rational and sound decisions. When it comes to money, the greatest emotion you or I display is the fear of losing it. And it is because of this fear that we often operate too safely and give our money away, or we jump in and jump right out if we lose a little bit of it. We have all experienced emotions that bypassed our rational brains and, as a result, missed out on an opportunity, or worse, failed altogether. This is why to have a high financial IQ, you must relinquish any emotional stimuli and learn to see the numbers with your mind and not your eyes.

## AM I REALLY DIVERSIFIED?

> *The most valuable thing I had was not the cash nor the property...It was the cash flow.*

> *- 'Freeway' Rick Ross*

Diversification has long been explained as having stock in different industries and sectors to protect an investor and spread the risk. However, is this a safe financial strategy to have or to offer someone? In reality, you are putting all of your money into one market, the stock exchange, and forgetting about all the other markets—real estate, physical gold and silver, and businesses (car wash, Laundromat, franchise, property management company, etc.). What happens if the stock market collapses as a whole but hard assets like physical gold, silver, and land increase? Will you be diversified then? I don't think so.

Many of us have been conditioned to think like a poor person. The buy, hold, and pray attitude no longer applies in this new economy. Investing in one asset class and feeling that you are diversified will subject you to the boom and bust cycles, creating a perpetual cycle of dependence on the system for survival. The rich, however, focus on the power of their asset column, i.e., businesses, real estate, paper assets, and commodities. They do not invest in only one market; they spread their risk across asset columns. This way, they can protect their wealth in the event of an economic downturn. In fact, the rich simply take their winnings and use the appreciation from them to buy more undervalued assets—assets that have been affected by a macroeconomic downturn. This is why you hear the term "the rich getting richer." They are getting richer because they are playing this kind of diversified game. They are diversifying their asset classes, not just their stocks.

## BARGAIN HUNT LIKE THE RICH

Many of us only shop for liabilities that are considered on sale, such as a nice car, exclusive sneakers, clothes, and jewelry. Although these items make us poorer and cost us money in the long run, we convince ourselves that this is the right way to bargain hunt and "save money." However, the wealthy approach to bargain shopping is completely different to that of the financially uneducated. The rich wait for pullbacks in the stock market and corrections in real estate and purchase these assets "on sale" as the herd begins to sell in fear. The rich also invest in assets such as businesses, gold and silver, and technologies that will be at the forefront in the future before people are made aware of it. If you don't believe me, here are two examples of how a savvy investor can capitalize on bargain shopping for assets:

1. Look at Jay-Z's acquisition of Tidal. While many artists were continuing to be paid a secure check from record executives and streaming services, Jay was bargain shopping for a streaming service of his own in Tidal. He was able to purchase the streaming service

company for about $53 million and almost triple his ROI in less than two years.

2. I know someone who shopped for Bitcoin on a bargain in 2010. He invested $100 while the price of the company was tremendously weak, and by 2014, he made over $77,000. Talk about bargain hunting and buying something "on sale." In just four years, he was able to increase his return exponentially just by bargain hunting and buying while assets were "on sale." He now has a few hundred dollars of the house's money scattered around different marijuana stocks. He is still bargain shopping.

You must learn to see what the financially uneducated are blinded by and bargain hunt for assets rather than liabilities. Unfortunately, the poor mentality tells us to shop for liabilities that are on sale. Let's start to bargain hunt like the rich and learn to buy assets that are on sale. This is a proven way to increase your wealth and build your income stream so that you can buy liabilities on sale with the profits from your acquired assets. This technique is how you amass a real fortune within our society.

# 9

# So You Want to Be a Millionaire, Huh?

We all want to be millionaires. But that dream always lasts until we get our first million. Instead of wanting to be a millionaire, ask yourself, "What kind of millionaire do I want to be?"

## WHICH WOULD YOU RATHER?

Let's play a quick game of "Would you rather." This game can help you better assess who you want to be as a millionaire and the mind-set you have to have in order to get there. Here goes:

1. *Would you rather* be a doctor or the owner of a pharmaceutical company?
2. *Would you rather* invest in stocks or own a hedge fund?
3. *Would you rather* be a professional athlete or be the owner of the sports team who signs the checks?

4. *Would you rather* make money on Instagram or build the next Instagram?
5. *Would you rather* own a million-dollar house or own a million units paying you fifty dollars per month in cash flow?

Asking yourself these simple questions can help you see both sides of the world and give you more options in your quest to become a millionaire. As you may know, there are four economic groups:

1. The poor: anyone earning below minimum wage
2. The middle class: anyone earning higher end wages (makes up to $500K a year after taxes)
3. The rich: anyone earning a million dollars or more a year
4. The ultra wealthy: anyone earning a million dollars or more a month in passive and portfolio income

## DIFFERENT TYPES OF MILLIONAIRES

### Millionaire #1—net worth:

If you are looking to have a high net worth, this is the spot for you. Net-worth millionaires are the largest group of millionaires and the fastest to become. This is due to the "perceived value" of what you own, as opposed to what you can get when you sell. Allow me to explain: Let's say you have a house that you bought for $300,000, and it's now worth $1.3 million. You are technically a net-worth millionaire, assuming your house sells at the valued price. Owning stocks can be another example if you have a million dollars' worth of stocks, bonds, retirement plans, or mutual funds. These millionaires may seem rich on paper. However, they have one problem. They are producing very little cash flow, and money is flowing out of their pockets to maintain the homes they live in. They still have to rely on working to maintain their lifestyle.

## Millionaire #2—high-paying job:

Are you interested in receiving a million-dollar paycheck or salary? How about only receiving $600,000 after taxes, even though you've earned or have done a million dollars of work? High-income wage earners are taxed at the highest rates today! Some of the people who fall into this bracket are CEOs, executives, professional athletes, actors, musicians, and lottery winners. Although they have a million-dollar income (which qualifies them as millionaires), they are one negative earnings report, severe injury, hit or miss, or bad economy away from losing their job and running out of money if they can't get another job for any reason.

### Millionaire #3—cash flow (money generated while sleeping):

Ah! Welcome to the graduate school of capitalism and finance. Do you have what it takes to produce a million dollars a month in cash flow (passive income)? The people in this category receive income from their assets. They don't have to earn a million-dollar salary to make a million dollars. This is why we see entrepreneurs like Jeff Bezos (founder of Amazon), Steve Jobs (founder of Apple), Mark Zuckerberg (founder of Facebook), and Larry Elson (Oracle) all take a salary of one dollar each year from their companies. In fact, the majority of the cash flow millionaires in the world are in the 1 percent and 0.01 percent. They don't have to labor or even think to produce cash flow from their assets every month. They just use that money from their existing assets and buy more assets with it. This is where you want to be—the no taxes, no liabilities, and no apologies club!

### A MILLION DOLLARS' WORTH OF GAME FOR $9.99

**Question:** *Why would the people with the most money choose to use someone else's?*

There is a big clue right there. If you want to become wealthy, then you have to do what wealthy people do. Wealthy people use debt to grow their wealth. They access as much debt or capital as they can in order to acquire assets. Corporations leverage debt all of the time with a view to acquire or merge with other companies. That is why we see record numbers in mergers & acquisitions during downward economies. When interest rates are low, multinational corporations directly borrow cheap money and use it to buy other multinational corporations, monopolizing industries and knocking out the competition.

> *Y'all think it's bougie, I'm like, it's fine. But I am trying to give you a million dollars' worth of game for $9.99.*

> —JAY-Z

The game is simple: you want to leverage as much good debt as you can to buy assets that pay you a positive cash flow, and once you have your wealth where you want it, eliminate the debt to preserve it. That's solid advice that you probably won't hear from the financial gurus populating our mainstream media. It makes me wonder if their advice is any good. If their advice to save money, pay down debt, buy, hold, and pray, or even to avoid debt is good advice, the advice that the masses adhere to, then why is 99 percent of the population forced to share 40 percent of the nation's income while the 1 percent has 60 percent of it? This is because the 99 percent focuses on saving money and paying down debt, while the 1 percent focuses on creating streams of money using other people's time and other people's money (debt). You can get rich using your money, but to gain wealth, you need to learn to use other people's money. I am pretty sure these "financial gurus" bought by the media are part of the 1 percent. They have created streams of money through selling us the advice to save money. Guess how I feel? Dumbo.

## IF YOU ADOPT STATUS QUO PRINCIPLES, YOU GET STATUS QUO RESULTS

If you want to be rich, you need to think independently rather than go along with the crowd. In doing what everyone does, my guess is you'll probably wind up having what everyone else has. This most likely means that a lifetime of debt, unfair taxes, and hard labor looms on your horizon. The reason why the 1 percent is a rare population is that they think differently from everyone else. If you want to join the ranks of the 1 percent, then you must retrain your mind to think like a wealthy person and learn to adopt the philosophies of the rich. In other words, "Don't work hard—work smart." Henry Ford, the founder of Ford Motors, once said that "thinking is the hardest work a person can do." I believe this is true. Thinking forces people to exercise brain muscles not usually utilized, which requires a ton of energy to do. This is why you hear the term "writer's block" or "being stuck in your head." Thinking requires a lot of work, but it allows you to connect with cognitive forces that will help spur innovation and creativity.

Becoming financially educated takes altering your thoughts about money and thinking independently. There are many distractions in this world like television, entertainment, drama, and social media that do not require us to exercise our cognitive abilities and think ingeniously. There are also salespeople posing as experts in any field who interfere with our ability to self-educate or even become financially literate. The only way to combat these cognitive distractions is to educate yourself and give yourself space and time just to think. Thinking about who you want to be, what you excel at, what problems you want to solve in the world, and who you want to spend your time with can change the outcome of your life substantially. So having space and the freedom to think can be the difference between reliance and independence.

## HOW MUCH DOES IT COST YOU PER DAY TO LIVE?

I remember my uncle sharing with me what his dad taught him about budgeting when he was a child. It was a pretty unusual method, as the traditional way to budget is to track monthly income and expenses. However, this strategy offered a new and creative way to help people stay on top of their finances. He told me to break my finances down to the day. In other words, "How much does it cost you, *per day*, to live?" Many of us will not have an answer for this question, but this is why I was so intrigued. Up until then, I had never asked myself how much it would cost to live each day. So I began to jot down every expense (both fixed and variable) that I had for the month and divided it by the number of days within that month. What I found was shocking. I came up with about $52 a day in total daily expenses. I did the same for income, and it came out to $102 per day of income; pretty good, I'd say, for not even knowing how much it cost me to live. After this exercise, he then told me to track how much money I was spending every day for a month—down to a stick of gum. This was a great exercise for me to find out what my guilty pleasures were and how much money I was spending unnecessarily that could have otherwise gone to saving and investing. This was a great lesson for me. It showed me how much money I had left on the table and how knowing this is the difference between being ahead and being behind on my finances. In doing this, you can find money that you didn't think you had and begin to invest your way to a million dollars with it.

## A DOLLAR AND A DREAM

I understand that when existing in poverty, sometimes all we have is a dollar and a dream. I also recognize that our dreams are often limited to our surroundings, but I'm here to provide a different perspective on ways to accumulate wealth. In my opinion, having limited resources is the foundation of innovation. This is because people who lack resources often have the ability to empathize with common problems faced by the masses and therefore can come up with creative solutions for these issues. It is even beneficial to learn how to build a business with as few resources as possible. That way, once you come into some money, you can think creatively and make your money go a long way instead of blowing it and running out of money trying to build a business. This is the main reason why businesses fail, in my opinion. Ninety-nine percent of all businesses fail within the first year of inception, not because they have a bad product or service or because of the entrepreneurs' incompetence, but only because the business runs out of money.

In the book *The Power of Broke*, Daymond John touches on the notion of how being broke forces you to tap into your creative mind and build a big business on a budget instead of reaching for your wallet to buy innovation to become successful as an entrepreneur. This is why I challenge you to consider what kind of millionaire you want to be as opposed to asking you if you want to be a millionaire. This exercise forces you to think creatively about different methods of creating wealth from nothing but an idea. If you can master creating money from your ideas, you will never have to depend on a job to survive. You will be able to be the job provider and value producer. Is this not why we all exist? To create value and help one another? This is the ultimate achievement in human evolution: the ability to create value for one another and make our lives in the world that much easier.

## HOW HIGH ARE YOU SETTING YOUR GOALS?

> You don't always have to be right. Just always be courageous.

> — JEREMIAH BROWN

Can I challenge you to do something? Great! What I want you to do is to set a goal so high and great that it may seem unattainable to not only your peers but to you as well. How does this challenge make you feel? Do you feel a bit of anxiety or nervousness? Do you doubt your capability and skill to achieve your goal? Or has society already told you who it thinks you are and what it thinks you're capable of? These are some of the things you should ask yourself as you begin to write down your goals. Sure, these emotions are natural and very understandable if you haven't started yet, but contrary to belief, achieving your goals is not what's important in life. What is more important is the journey to get there and who you become as a result. We all subconsciously place caps on the height of our goals. These caps can often be viewed as shields against failure, disappointment, and embarrassment.

I want you to imagine the worst-case scenario in regard to your most profound, idealistic goals. Envision setting a goal to reach a billion dollars in cash flow while doing what you love, giving back to your community, and empowering the people around you. Now, think about what you will have or land on if you don't meet these goals. Are you a failure if you don't reach your goals but earn $50,000 doing what you love and serving your community the best you can? I don't think so, and neither should you. The point I am trying to make is that you have to aim for the stars if you desire to land on the moon. You have to set extremely high goals and work diligently to achieve them. However, if you fail to make it, you will still be abundantly blessed once you understand where you are compared to where you started.

If your goal is to achieve wealth in a capitalist nation like America, you should change your thoughts around your goals and heighten your goals. Instead of setting a goal to obtain a billion dollars, set a goal that centers on serving people. Tell yourself that you want to help and serve a billion people, and the money will follow. In doing this, you will have a clear understanding of the industries and groups of people that you want to serve and provide value for. Setting goals like the ones mentioned are a sure way to achieve wealth. If you are affecting lives and offering value, then society will compensate you in in many ways.

## FOR MY CORPORATE EMPLOYEES (INTRAPRENEURS)

Your boss cannot make you rich. In fact, it is not his or her job to do so. Your boss's job is to ensure you get your paycheck and bonus. The real difference between you and a millionaire is not what you earn but what you spend your money on and do in your spare time.

# Financial Freedom: *My Only Hope*

Even if you are a VP or C-level executive of a Fortune 500 company, even if you earn over $750,000 before taxes and net close to $400,000 annually, if your expenses match or exceed your income, you will quickly see how this strategy will yield a negative result for you. You will struggle financially if you go down this path. Instead of using the money you make to buy "stuff"—cars, boats, and other high-end items—converting a portion of your money into assets that pay you outside of work can be the remedy to financial struggle. I am pretty sure there are people in this position who earn a high salary but spend more than they earn and buy liabilities that they think are assets. If you want to achieve financial freedom, then you need to think like a producer rather than a consumer. It is one thing to earn money, but it's another to keep it and have the money you earn make more money for you. As mentioned before, there are many ways to print money legally and leverage what you have to buy assets that produce cash flow. It is this technique that separates the middle class from the ultrarich.

## BLUE-COLLAR MILLIONAIRE

You do not have to work in corporate America to gain wealth. I have a mentor who became a millionaire working as a corrections officer. He started working there at the age of twenty-two and has been at the same job ever since. He invested his after-tax earnings into cash-flowing properties. He earned an average salary of about $60K per year and purchased two properties each year for ten years. He delayed the instant gratification of buying high-end cars and jewelry and bought property instead. In the end, he had over a million dollars in equity along with $7,000 in monthly income from his rental properties. His salary also increased within those ten years of working. He now brings home right under $12,000 a month. He is on the fast track to reaching financial freedom. Not bad for a thirty-two-year-old.

There are many ways to set yourself free financially outside of your corporate or blue-collar job. It shouldn't matter how far you climb up the corporate ladder or how much you love your job or profession; having income coming in from outside your workspace will help ease the anxiety about an unforeseen circumstance like an economic downturn, layoff, shift in management, or glass ceiling. Investing your money wisely and understanding taxation in a wage-earning versus a pass-through entity can be the difference in not only how much you make but how much of that money you keep and have working for you. It is time to change the game from working for money to having money work for you while you enjoy what you do. The ability to focus on the task at hand increases productivity in the workforce because it allows people to shift the focus from lack of money to providing real and positive value in society. This advice will allow you to accumulate the wealth you need outside of the workplace so that you can focus on being selfless as opposed to selfish.

## FRUGALITY IS FREEDOM

Frugality is more about making distinctions between things that matter and things that don't matter than it is about saving money. Being frugal is a discipline that requires a strong sense of equanimity and EQ. It is also the closest thing to financial freedom. Once you make the connection between frugality and financial freedom, you are on your way to reaching millions. Frugality allows another friend of mine to get away with working less than eight hours a week. He makes thirty dollars an hour, but he saves 40 percent of his income to invest, and the rest goes to living expenses—food, shelter, and water. This may sound like a nightmare until you hear that he is able to take three trips to exotic locations a year. Even better, the cash flow that he receives from his investments is funding these trips, and he mentioned that it took him five years to set himself up like this financially.

# 10

# Silver Rights

*You cannot legislate goodness, and you cannot pass*
*a law to force someone to respect you. The only way*
*to social justice in a capitalist country is through*
*economic parity and ownership.*

—Dr. Martin Luther King

Financial literacy, ownership, and collaborative economics are the swords that we need to combat social and economic inequality. I believe that every minority in the world should learn how to be an entrepreneur even if he or she is working for someone else. I say this because financial power is about creating generational wealth and opportunities. Can you give your position in corporate America to your children? Sure, you may be able to introduce them to recruiters, but whether your child gets the job or not depends on the recruiter of the company bringing your child in, not you.

I never understood why we complain about rising unemployment rates and lack of income, ownership, and opportunities in a country that was predominately built for another culture to thrive in. It is the equivalent of going into someone's home and being upset that the inhabitants didn't offer you any of their food. Sure, providing food in the form of economic opportunity would be a moral and courteous thing to do, but it's not your home to make those demands. My solution is to build your own home! Start your own businesses, invest, learn to see each other as assets rather than liabilities, and collaborate with one another. Minorities have been conditioned to see a person who looks like them as inferior. This cognitively reinforced viewpoint separates people within these communities and creates little to no economic activity and mobility as a result. Besides, it's probably easier for minority communities to build a job then it is to find one.

## ABRAHAM LINCOLNOMICS

All that anyone seems to remember about Abraham Lincoln's freedom movement was the Emancipation Proclamation Act of 1863. However, what is kept under wraps from the history books is an act that he passed on March 3, 1865. President Lincoln signed into law the Freedmen's Bureau Act, which enabled Lincoln to set up the Freedman's Bank. The Freedman's Bank's mission was to teach freed slaves about money and the free enterprise system. This act may not seem that radical, but think about this—the president of the United States thought that the most transformational thing he could do for freed slaves after physical slavery was to teach them about the language of money and give them access to capital to help finance the four hundred thousand acres (forty acres and a mule) of land that was promised to them. This gesture was radical two hundred years ago and most likely contributed to his assassination. He was killed five weeks later on April 16, 1865.

Lincoln placed the Freedmen's Bureau Act so high on his priority list that he put the Freedman's Bank right across from the White House. That bank today is Bank of America, and you can find it near the White House. Following Lincoln's death, a new regime of white supremacy took hold and infiltrated every part of the banking system, including the Freedman's Bank. The bank eventually collapsed due to reckless speculation and gambling by these bankers. At the time of the collapse, there were close to seventy thousand black depositors who lost all of their money and assets. These were former slaves who believed in the free enterprise system so much that they, after slavery, were willing to take part in it in hopes of financial freedom. Frederick Douglas invested his $10,000 ($1 million in today's currency) into the bank to restore it. His initiative to revive the bank failed, and he lost his money as a result. He mentioned that "the failure of the bank did more to set freed slaves back than ten more years of slavery."

## GAVE US LEMONS

It is important that you know why we are in this economic position today. We never got the memo about the importance and power of financial literacy. If you are curious to know why black and other minority communities fail to progress in this economic system, this, along with harsher agendas, can be considered the reason. There was a time in history when African Americans would have been killed for learning how to read books or even participating in the free enterprise system. There were and still are tight restrictions that tried to prevent this disenfranchised community from achieving a collaborative and thriving financial ecosystem, but this regal community overcame and blossomed. This group of minorities was given lemons, sour, unripe lemons, that in time and with resourcefulness, they turned into lemonade. Although this is very impressive given the limited time and resources that were available, now it is time that we own the lemonade stand.

> *In the past twenty-five years, we've made dumb sexy...It is now the time to rebuild the image of black culture and black economics.*
>
> *- JOHN HOPE BRYANT*

There has also been a shift in our culture within the past few decades. This change or enlightenment had to take place for this newfound power to ensue The culture that once glorified struggle and made dumb sexy is now turning to a new frontier, education and entrepreneurship, to liberate the masses and set a new tone for Afrocentric royalty. Black people are begging to understand the power in ownership and credit as it relates to economic advancement within society. Before, black people had to rely on a biased financial, justice, and corporate system to survive. Now, these kings and queens are building systems, infiltrating these historically difficult structures, and providing social and economic opportunities for their communities. I predict that within the next three decades, there will be quadruple the number of black billionaires that there are now. The billionaires of today are laying the path and setting the example (good or bad) for the next wave of entrepreneurial leaders. This shift in culture will drastically change the game for all minorities and create an even playing field within society. Once we dominate, we will help out other cultures and races and show the wealthy of today how it is really done. We will become capitalists with hearts, social engineers, and show our divine empathy and compassion. This is real leadership, and I believe that is our task from up above. This is why our plight has been challenging and tempestuous.

## ENDING "YOUR" POVERTY

"Ending 'your' poverty" is not marketing talk that deals with ways to combat poverty and economic deprivation. No, instead of focusing on a macro level, I am going to start person to person. I believe that if you want real-world results, you have to relate to ordinary people and think in the real world. And if that means focusing on ending "your" poverty first, then so be it.

There are four major factors within your control that aid in your ability to end your own poverty. These factors are the following:

- Hope
- Education
- Self-esteem
- Role models

## HOPE

Ending your poverty starts with hope. Hope is so strong that you only need 5 percent of it to change your life! Hope is like an engine to a car. You can have a Bentley, but if the engine doesn't work, then the car is worthless and stuck. Hope can take on many forms, including ambition, determination, aspiration, and faith. Having hope allows you to think clearly and understand the simple fact that where you are today will not determine where you will be tomorrow. With hope, you take back the power of your circumstances and gain control of your destiny. This simple choice can change your entire trajectory in life, even if it's one that you are not satisfied with. Whether you run, walk, or crawl, with hope as your inner compass, you will progress. This is why this powerful yet simple four-letter word is the first step to ending your poverty.

## EDUCATION

Another tool that can be used to end your poverty is education. Education is derived from the Latin word "educe" and means to "bring out or develop something." That is what education really means. However, our society misinterprets the definition and instead indoctrinates us into a system rather than drawing out our inner genius. Education can come in many forms, including reading, real-world simulation, experience, observation, and failure. Failure and observation are sometimes the best ways to educate yourself in life. This helps you understand what doesn't work, what you are and aren't good at, and what your real purpose is in life. But all too often, school teaches you that failing spells the end of your future and your ability to progress financially in life. School also teaches you that failing a test or a course proves your inadequacy in society and reinforces your stupidity in a particular subject or category. This negative reinforcement ultimately blocks you from understanding where your genius lies, and we all have a "gen-i-in-us" waiting to propel us to financial freedom. Self-education is the only way to tap into your genius and draw out who you are meant to be in this world.

## SELF-ESTEEM

*Ninety percent of confidence is preparation…*
*Everything else is beyond your control.*

-RICHARD KLINE.

Self-esteem can be the driving force that enables you to execute your goals and live out your dreams. Self-esteem can also impact every other aspect of your life, from the choices you make and the people you surround yourself with to how you determine your self-worth within society. Understanding your value proposition as it pertains to self-esteem can determine your ability to accomplish your goals and achieve your dreams. Have you ever felt like you didn't belong in a particular group, job, school, or community? These feelings can be caused by low self-esteem or the fact that you don't feel worthy enough to exist in that space. You are a circle trying to fit into a puzzle of squares, wondering why you don't fit in or measure up. Sure, you can nip and tuck your "circle," suppressing what makes you unique to assimilate, but how will you find your true purpose? More importantly, are you not willing to discover who you are? I can see how systematic rules, media portrayals, public perception, and negative societal reinforcement can affect one's self-esteem and enhance the negative perception of self. But assimilating to society is not a remedy for low self-esteem, and it can even be harmful to your mental health in the long term.

*If you don't believe in yourself at 9 in the morning,*
*by 9 pm somebody is going to tell you who you are.*

—JOHN HOPE BRYANT

I believe high self-esteem derives from self-discovery and belief in oneself. If you start believing in your differences and subtle nuances, you will start to see your value in society and exploit it. Whether the value you have to offer is niche or on a global scale, every one of us can impact lives and effect change within society. High self-esteem or self-confidence helps you discover your gifts and enables you to share these gifts with society. As we know, half of success is confidence and belief in yourself. Think of high self-esteem as the food that gives you energy. We all need this energy to do anything in life. Look at self-esteem as a way to express what you have to offer the world and understand that you are important and you do have a purpose. Having high self-esteem will draw out your purpose, making the world a better place to be in because you're here.

## ROLE MODELS

Role models may be the last component to ending your own poverty, but I assure you, this too is very important. I remember going to business school and asking many of my classmates why they chose business and finance as their topic of focus. All of them said the reason behind their choice was because they either witnessed their or their friends' dads being successful businessmen or saw someone who looked like them as a successful businessman through the media or television screen. This put a lot of things in perspective for me. It taught me that kids in affluent communities were no smarter than I was. They were only modeling what they saw growing up. This is very important because all too often, the only things shown as signs of success for minorities in inner city communities are sports, entertainment, and illegal accumulation of wealth. I still applaud any way of bootstrapping your way out of poverty and becoming successful in life. However, there are far easier and less stressful ways of achieving wealth and success in this world.

*If you hang around 9 broke people, you will be the 10th.*

Role modeling can also encompass the people you spend most of your time with. Entrepreneur and recording artist 50 Cent agrees with this premise. He said, "You are as good as the people you speak to for no reason." Even though you have no control over who birthed you or your background, you do have control over whom you spend your time with. You should work on spending time with people you want to learn from, even if you aren't able to physically hang out with them. I have many billionaire mentors that I have never seen in person. I do, however, spend time listening to them and learning their strategies on how to achieve success and become wealthy. The difference between myself and most people is that I spend a lot of my free time reading their work and learning their moves, while other people spend their free time watching people who won't offer any applicable value to them other than a laugh or entertainment. So if you want to be successful, align yourself both physically and digitally with successful people in the field you want to be successful in. This strategy can aid in your ability to achieve success and knowledge.

## WE NEED MORE ENTREPRENEURS AND SMALL-BUSINESS OWNERS

In the past few years, there have been more small business deaths than there were births. Many aspiring entrepreneurs have no way of accessing capital due to sterner regulations and laws being passed, making it harder than ever before to take out credit to fund an endeavor. This, along with the rise of technology, will bring an end to small businesses and as a result spell doom for the American way of life. These deaths are mainly attributed to the rise of multinational corporations and the reignition of a monopoly throughout these big corporations. With the help of economic down-turns and the Federal Reserve, large businesses can leverage cheap money (debt) to merge with other industry giants and knock out the little man—mom and pop shops. And it looks like things aren't changing anytime soon. The only way that we can control our destiny is if we begin to support and invest in each other through crowd-funding and collaborative economics.

Here are some relevant facts that show the impact of small businesses:

- There are 350 million people (and counting) in America.
- There are over 27 million businesses in America.
- Only 970 out of 27 million businesses in America employ 10,000 people or more.
- **50 percent of all employment in America involves 100 employees or less.**

There is a reason that the last statistic is in bold. Small businesses are the backbone of our economy and the largest employers in every community. Think about the last time you visited the dentist, got a haircut, or went to a restaurant to eat. I am pretty sure you saw more than eight employees in every place you went. Now, have you ever wondered why large corporations' stock prices increase whenever they announce significant reductions in their work force (mass firing)? This is because they are rewarded for maximizing profits at any cost, including laying off their workers.

There should be an income cap in capitalism—whether individual or corporate income, if it exceeds a certain amount, it should immediately go into an escrow account (funded by a private organization) that then supports entrepreneurs or small businesses.

## COLLABORATIVE ECONOMICS

Black Wall Street was the first example of how powerful and fruitful the effect of collaborative economics could be. Taking advantage of the oil booms in the early 1900s allowed a group of marginalized people to reignite a collaborative economy not seen since the beginning of the African dynasties of Timbuktu and ancient Egypt. Just to show how successful the people there were, some records illustrate that the dollar was circulated close to a hundred times before leaving the community. In comparison, it takes the dollar no more than twenty times to circulate before leaving white and Asian communities today. It also took close to a year on average before the dollar left the community during black wall street. Talk about keeping it in the community!

The people of Black Wall Street were extremely prosperous and focused. Many of them understood the role they played within society and played it well. There were black attorneys, business owners, PhDs, and doctors alike who lived and worked within the communities they shared. One doctor was Dr. Berry, who owned the bus system. His average income was $500 a day—in 1910! That illustrious amount today would easily exceed $13,000 per day in today's currency. The same amount of money can be generated today. However, it would probably be spent on items not owned by the community in which the money was made to begin with. In spending money outside the community, a Black Wall Street–like economy is further disrupted, set back, and not able to continue.

Collaborative economics has more to do with building dynasties than it does with buying products within your community. Entire ecosystems are built through the power of using nepotism, buying real estate, and investing in entrepreneurship within your community. These simple practices can transform any impoverished or disenfranchised population into an affluent and royal civilization. However, to act on these principles, the following cognitive steps have to take place:

1. Change the mentality from inferiority to self-confidence
2. Relinquish dependency upon foreign communities
3. Dismantle the "one at a time" or "less is more" mentality
4. Understand the power of heritage

I can only imagine how quickly an empire could be built by putting these cognitive models into practice. This will work and has worked for all communities who applied these principles in the construction of self-sustaining, self-reliant, and thriving societies. To economically shift a community, the people in it must collaborate and work together. No one man (or woman) is an island. We all need each other to create a self-sufficient society again.

## COLORLESS: WHEN SOMETHING'S GOOD, IT GOES WAY BEYOND COLOR

Sports and entertainment can be a prime example of something breaking through the color barrier. These industries have done more to bridge the gap in race relations than any other industry or social movement today. Sports and entertainment enable people of all different colors, creeds, religions, and backgrounds to exist in one space, have the same "mental complexity" and similar commonalities, and even do business together. We see this in legendary basketball star Michael Jordan and icon Beyoncé being household names in every race and in a corporate conglomerate like Apple purchasing a minority co-owned company for $3 billion: Beats by Dre. Although inherent prejudice still holds humanity back from achieving ultimate innovation, industries and brands like the ones mentioned can grow exponentially and reach everyone simply because the tone and value are universal.

As we progress in society, we will start to see the rise in technology and entrepreneurship bridge the gap between race relations throughout society. Robert F. Smith, Tristan Walker, and Bozoma Saint John are all prime examples of this.

With the creation of his innovative hair product Bevel, Tristan Walker has been able to raise capital ($24 million) from not only minority-owned venture funds but unlikely juggernaut venture capital funds such as Andreessen Horowitz and Google Ventures. Although Silicon Valley has been traditionally seen as excluding diversity from the boardrooms and discriminating based on age among other things, Tristan did not let this stop him from offering value to the world. He not only has been able to participate and thrive within the Silicon Valley community, but he was able to do it in his twenties! With Tristan's intellect, business prowess, and fearlessness, he can prove to everyone that value creation and innovation can be the spear that pierces through the color barrier.

If there is anybody badass enough to revolutionize not only marketing but the perception of a boardroom, then Bozoma Saint John is the right person to do it. Fierce, brash confident, poised, and competitive are terms given to Fortune 500 CEOs and billionaires, but as an C-level executive, Bozoma can sashay around these adjectives like a prom queen at her last dance. Although many of you may have witnessed her introduction to stardom from her appearances at WWDC and Uber, the fascinating part of the story was her rise to get there. Boz has shown through her hard work, confidence, business acumen, persistence, and resilience that impossible is nothing but a ten-letter word. She has created enough value to be considered an asset by some of the top players in the industry, from Jimmy Iovine to Apple's CEO, Tim Cook, and Uber's cofounder, Garrett Camp. Bold, black, and beautiful are the three Bs that have enabled Boz to rise up the corporate ladder and be respected among some of the greatest executives ever to do so. She is a proven example of something being so good that it breaks through the racial and color barrier.

Robert F. Smith, CEO and founder of private equity firm Vista Equity Partners, has been dubbed by the *Washington Post* and *Forbes* as "the quiet billionaire," and this description couldn't be closer to the truth. Even his website appears to have no picture of him on it. Many of you probably have not heard of the private equity financier, but he has done more to change the perception of the black community than we can ever imagine. As if building a $26 billion business of buying, growing, and selling software isn't impressive enough, Robert was able to thrive in this business and climb the ranks to billionaire stature as a black man. He was able to accomplish this goal ingeniously. Robert chose to stay under the radar publicly as he focused on adding value for his clients behind the scenes. He believed that investors and executives should know him first by his abilities. If they saw only the caramel skin of an African American, he would have lost out on many opportunities to grow his business and increase his wealth. Instead, he let his business talk for him. Creating value and money, of course, turned out to be the only color that the market saw. Robert is a brilliant mind who was able to create value for many different people from many diverse backgrounds. This is because he understood the human experience. He recognized that everyone, white, black, red, or blue, is looking for one thing: value.

**Side note:** Robert F. Smith also extends his philanthropic efforts to the communities from which he came. From being one of the largest donors to the African American Museum to being the founding president of multiple nonprofit groups that focus on African American culture, human rights, music education, and the environment, Robert Smith has proven that participating in the free market cannot and should not force you to turn your back on your community in order to stay ahead.

Here is a list of many other compelling examples of black game changers:

- Sean "Puffy" Combs
- Sean Carter
- Percy Lavon Julian
- Percy "Master P" Miller
- Oprah Winfrey
- Mansa Musa
- Louis Farrakhan
- Reginald Lewis
- Steve Stoute
- Dr. Boyce Watkins
- Barack and Michelle Obama
- Cathy Hughes

- Dr. Dre
- Sophia Stewart
- Martin Luther King Jr.
- Muhammad Ali
- Floyd Mayweather
- Malcolm X and Tupac Shakur
- Prince
- Bob Johnson
- Madam C. J. Walker
- (Your name here)

I hope that these powerful examples of greatness breaking through the color barrier can change your views and the considerations you have about your reality. If these people can fearlessly infiltrate these historically racially dismissive industries, then we all have the power to do the same. You just have to find your inner genius and leverage it to serve others and provide value throughout the world. I know this may seem a bit cliché, but it is an incredibly true statement: "Give, and you shall receive." The more lives you affect, the wealthier you will become. If you can empathize with all humanity, you will be able to find chinks in the world's iron armor and create a service around these chinks. I hope you understand that a system can try and dim your light all that it wants. However, once you are enlightened, once you educate yourself and start to believe in your abilities to create value for the world, then you will release your divine light. And no form of human engineering can stop God's light from shining. You have that light in you. It takes education, will, and a belief that you have all the tools you need to create value for others.

## JORDAN AND YEEZY

You guys probably think that you know where I am going with this topic, but I see both sides of each coin in life. So instead of chastising you about the "shiny things" known as Jordans or Yeezy Boosts sneakers, I am going to help you understand how to make money and still wear any of the designer clothes that you like.

Listen, I came from the inner city, and I can certainly understand the power of wearing some popping Js on your feet or even Yeezy boosts with shorts. The problem, in my opinion, is not the fact that we all are wearing them, but the fact that we are not buying them wisely. There is such a dramatic increase in the price of these sneakers in the aftermarket. I would never pay the "Johnny price" (aftermarket price) for sneakers. That is just plain theft to me. Instead, I would turn myself into an entrepreneur and sell one pair of the sneakers for double the initial price. That way, I would recoup my initial investment and still have a nice pair of kicks to wear. Therefore, I would recommend buying two pairs on the release date. One pair can be for you to wear, and the other pair can be the pair that you flip to make up for the money spent buying both. This is how I would leverage buying sneakers.

If you can't afford to get two pairs, then you probably shouldn't be buying these kinds of sneakers. But even if you can't afford it, partnering with a friend or relative can work as well. Doing this is the equivalent to buying a stock on a margin call in the stock market. You tell your mom, friend, or brother that you have enough for one pair but need to borrow enough cash to cover the other pair. You flip the other pair for double the initial price and pay the money back with interest. Therefore, you now have one pair of Jordan or Yeezy sneakers along with a few extra bucks for you to invest in Nike and Adidas stock. This way, Jordan and Yeezy can now start paying you.

## THE RISE OF CRYPTOCURRENCY

I am pretty sure we've all heard in the news that if we'd invested five dollars in Bitcoin a few years back, we'd be almost $5 million richer today. It is hard to believe, but Bitcoin is one of many different cryptocurrencies in existence today. It is, however, the most famous one, so I am only going to focus on Bitcoin as the main form of cryptocurrency. Bitcoin was created in 2008 as a peer-to-peer electronic cash system. This currency was designed to reduce corruption in our monetary system and restore order in the free market. Although this has proven effective, this area is so new that no one is sure what the downsides could be yet. Still, there is a huge network of people using this currency with success and reaping the benefits of its expansion and popularity. A lot of governments have also taken interest, and even China says it is looking at this form of commerce as a way to pull away from fiat currency.

There are a few benefits to this new cryptocurrency. These advantages include the following:

- No centralized power—controlled by the people
- Secure—trust is built into the blockchain
- More efficient—faster transactions
- Easy entry—anyone can buy and trade Bitcoin
- Inflation proof—you can't print this currency

## SHOULD I INVEST?

So let's get to the real question: Should you invest? Well, the answer is that it depends on what you are looking for. Are you seeking to invest in cryptocurrency for the long term? Will you be using it like gold—as a store of value and a hedge against any financial crisis that may ensue (and we all know that financial crisis is inevitable due to currency printing)? If so, then the choice is yours to make. There are two strategies that people can take to approach this safely:

1. Buy when the price goes down, accumulate more, and never sell until years down the road.
2. Speculate—which I only advise if you are an expert in this space or don't mind losing money to earn it.

As cryptocurrency involves a real free market outside of our current one, buying to speculate may be a bad strategy for this type of phenomenon. I'd personally stick to acquiring hard assets like real estate and land, since you need a medium of exchange to buy it. It does not matter what the government decides to do in regard to commerce and currency. But whatever it chooses to rule as currency will need to be used for someone to buy my property from me. I am sticking to items that require money and will be a hedge against any form of inflation and currency change, and that is land and real estate.

## DO YOU LOVE ME, MARY JANE?

I want to take a quote from the late-seventies R&B song "Mary Jane" by Rick James to sum up the hardships associated with this precarious plant. "Do you love me, Mary Jane?" Do you really love us, marijuana? You have put us through hell and back in the past, sending us to prison, creating a bad stigma around our association with you, and even hiding your life-altering cures and treatments! So how can you expect us to trust you now? Even more, why are you working with the same people who rejected you and deprived you of your ability to change lives physically and economically in the first place? Maybe you are just as confused about us as we are about you. Only time will tell if you can liberate us from our economic plight and create a new wave of millionaire and billionaire entrepreneurs.

There has been a fear about investing and taking part in this marijuana "gold rush" for some time now. Although the revenue numbers are exponential and opportunities for expansion and growth are endless, many investors are still sitting on the sidelines waiting for the right time to jump into this industry. People see the risk of the federal government not allowing it and wonder whether or not it is going to change its stance in the future. The success of the industry is heavily tied to political control, as marijuana is legal in many states but illegal federally. What this means is that the federal government can come in at any time and take away a marijuana business if it sees fit. Also, African Americans are still getting lengthy sentences for distribution of marijuana while

CEOs and founders of marijuana companies are not. Have we been strategically stopped from entering this space? After all, this is our domain. We've mastered the art of business, sales, and distribution within this industry. So why aren't minorities prospering from this "gold rush"? Are minorities being legally kept from competing in this space?

In my opinion, marijuana will be the final frontier of wealth generation for minority communities. Once this industry becomes legal, minority entrepreneurs will have had enough experience and mastery in this space to be able to build a big business around it. As it becomes corporatized and regulated, I think that many people will be late to the party. However, this does not mean that people will not be able to amass millions and billions. I am saying that it will be more challenging to do so. In the event that marijuana becomes federally legal, we will start to see a surge of minorities accumulating massive amounts of wealth from this industry. There are many resources out there about building a legal marijuana enterprise that will help guide you into the niche you want to take part in. My advice to you is to learn about the business and how to get into it legally. This way, by the time it becomes legal on the federal level, you will have developed enough knowledge to build a turnkey operation generating millions.

## Financial Freedom: *My Only Hope*

### WHOEVER CONTROLS THE MONEY CONTROLS INNOVATION

Sadly, the social and economic divide and inequality in our society have really impacted capitalism for minority entrepreneurs, and this in turn has created a new term called "controlled capitalism." This is where bankers, hedge funds, venture capital firms, and investment groups make decisions as to what is and isn't considered innovative and investable. Controlled capitalism now means that these financial gatekeepers have switched from investing in a profitable product or service to investing in an entrepreneur or person. One of the issues that have always faced entrepreneurs of color is the lack of available capital to help them go into business or maintain a business. For the vast majority of the deals, either they have to like the entrepreneur or the entrepreneur has to be a good cultural fit or an investment to be made—whatever that means. Just take a look at today's entrepreneur television shows. There have been times when minority entrepreneurs would have great financials and be in lucrative industries but would not receive any funding to grow their businesses. On the other hand, white counterparts who had mediocre financials and sometimes no revenue whatsoever would be given a chance and be funded. Entrepreneurs of color will have a far better chance getting the capital needed to buy a car than they would for a business loan, even if the business is profitable.

I've even read technology articles reporting that some people consider hiring and investing in more minority start-ups to be "lowering standards" or even "charity work." There needs to be an awakening in collaborative economics if we want to even the platform and close the economic gap throughout the world.

## CONTROLLING YOUR OWN INNOVATION

There has been an emergence of crowd-funding that enables start-ups to bypass the financial gatekeepers and get the necessary capital to grow. My guess is that as we start to see this new industry of collaborative economies grow, there will be an advancement within our communities, as well as a newfound Trust within these communities as the industry continues to be successful in getting access to capital. I hope you are playing a role in helping your fellow minority start-ups get to scale. The survival and progression of cultures in need of money are dependent on your ability to trust and believe in them, regardless of the color of their skin, personal background, and social or economic upbringing. We need you to continue to push the culture of humanity forward. Are you up for the challenge?

## AFRO TECH—WHAT'S THE BILLIONAIRE HOLDUP?

Since the revolution in technology, there has been a rise in black and other minority tech founders and engineers. However, the lack of funding and opportunity throughout the tech industry has been outrageously high and ubiquitous. This makes me wonder: What is the holdup with the inception of tech billionaires being people of color? Are people of color purposely being stopped from scaling their companies and reaching a mass market? Or is it that these groups of entrepreneurs just aren't capable of creating that much value? My guess is the former. There are, however, solutions and new incubation happening today that will remedy this economic exclusion. Let me share a few incubators with you. If you have built a start-up or are interested in entering in the tech space, here is a list of early-stage and other venture capital firms and incubators that can serve you:

1. *DIGITALUNDIVIDED*
   Since black and Latina women are the fastest-growing group of entrepreneurs in the United States, Digitalundivided focuses on this demographic, providing seed capital and mentorship for entrepreneurs as they navigate through the industry.
2. *500 STARTUPS*
   500 Startups created a micro-fund that invests in black and Latino companies and provides founders with access to capital, networks, and entrepreneurial expertise.

3. *NEWME*

   The founder and CEO of NewME Accelerator, Angela Benton, is a dynamic VC who aims to accelerate, educate, and empower underrepresented tech entrepreneurs around the world.

4. *BACKSTAGE CAPITAL*

   Backstage Capital builds woman, LGBT, Hispanic, and minority tech companies. Founder Arlan Hamilton believes in funding teams from underrepresented backgrounds as a way to provide a competitive edge within the tech industry and produce returns comparable to traditional tech companies.

5. *BROOKLYN BRIDGEVENTURES*

   Brooklyn Bridge Ventures manages $23 million across two funds and focuses on later-stage companies (companies with revenue exceeding $5,000 per month).

With the emergence of incubators and venture capital firms like the ones mentioned that focus on growing and nurturing start-ups owned by people of color and underrepresented communities, you will see a shift in economic growth and prosperity in these communities in less than a decade. What is the holdup, you say? The holdup is not that we are being excluded from the tech revolution but the fact that we aren't investing in these companies that are focused on investing in start-ups within our communities. Let's get in this game. We should pool our money together and start more venture funds that will fund minority start-ups and provide jobs while transforming the economic future of our communities. It is up to us to build us!

# 11

# More Than Money

Although we may all agree that money makes the world go round, there are, in fact, other things that are worth more than money and will define whether a person is equipped to reach financial freedom. Equanimity, humility, swagger, integrity, and gratitude are all signs of true self-mastery. These are the some of the many traits you must have in order to achieve not only financial freedom but lifelong positive relationships and happiness. Having adopted a mentality of "greed is good," prejudice, and scarcity has moved many people in society away from realizing the ultimate human experience. These learned traits have instead created a life of chaos and hardships for all of us—including rich, poor, black, white, and many more. This chapter will show you how adopting simple principles and standards can separate you from the masses and create a sense of self-actualization in regard to your pursuit of wealth, success, and happiness.

## WHAT IS YOUR NUMBER?

Unfortunately, there are no guarantees that we will survive until the consensus retirement age or that the same rules of money (rates, regulations, and macroeconomics) will apply once we get to retirement. In order to achieve a financially free retirement, you must have a number in mind regarding the money you wish to accumulate as opposed to having an appropriate age range that you will retire at. This is because this fairy-tale notion of working and saving until you are sixty-five years of age ignores one rule of humanity: *we are all different and have different circumstances in life.* Having an "age cap" for retirement is like playing a game of musical chairs, and we know there always has to be one or two people standing at the end of that game. What if you are the one standing? This is why instead of having a cap for your age, you should set a number in mind that will allow you to live financially free. Doing this will not only make you stress-free as you begin to approach that age but will give you the discipline and clarity you need in order to reach your goal for retirement.

Having a number can apply to so many things outside of retirement. Let's name a few here:

1. Negotiating business deals
2. Negotiating salaries
3. Integrity—having a cap on what you are willing to do in order to get paid
4. Morality—how much money do you really need in life?

## PROUD WINDOW-SHOPPER

I remember going to open houses and exotic car dealerships looking at things that I couldn't afford and negotiating great deals that I knew could not close. I did this so that I could be savvy in the marketplace once I could afford it. I say this not to spark a wave of time wasters and window-shoppers but to point out that even if you have the money, shopping around for the right deal can save you thousands, if not millions, in the long run. Oftentimes, due to embarrassment and pressure by salesman, we give up our ability to find great deals within any marketplace. We adopt this "consumer mentality" and spend on demand rather than adopting a "producer mind-set" and shopping for the right deals *before* we begin to spend our hard-earned money.

# Financial Freedom: *My Only Hope*

Refusing to shop around before you buy and seeing deals with your emotion and not through your mind creates an enormous amount of buyer's remorse and subjects you to being deceived, defrauded, and even financially robbed! Buying without the proper knowledge of what is or isn't a good deal is not financially intelligent.

Take this, for instance:

You know how that new iPhone or that new car doesn't seem so new a year after you purchase it? Or how you always want the newest item that comes out after you already purchased the previous generation of it? Well, that is because your brain is hardwired to adapt, so you are used to what you bought, even if what you bought is still new. This repetitive chase of materialism and pleasure puts you in a never-ending cycle and drains you of all the money you have, putting it into the hands of your masters—the producers who sell it to you.

Remember this: we love the idea of buying more than buying itself. My advice to you is that if you ever get the urge to spend or have money burning a hole in your wallet, window-shop first (without money on you, of course). Only when you come across a win-win scenario, meaning something you like that is a good deal, should you pull the trigger and buy it!

## SWAGGER AND INTEGRITY

Allow me to share with you why swagger and integrity are correlated and why it is imperative that you incorporate these traits into who you are. These characteristics force you into something called "oneness of self." This means that you aren't willing to people-please, ignore the truth, or sell your soul or your community for a check, regardless of how high the stakes or numbers are. These traits require a sense of mental equanimity and deep, spiritual understanding in yourself and your abilities. They also prevent any interferences that will block you from your blessings and true purpose. Let us delve deeper:

**Integrity:** There was a time in history when all two people needed was a handshake in order to come to an agreement or solidify a deal in business. Today, a simple handshake is rarely sufficient. We have gone from a society of trust to one that requires law to create checks and balances between industry experts and clients looking for great service, help, or advice. We have noticed a rise in Ponzi schemes, bad customer service and experiences, and a lack of transparency altogether from the businesses and services we depend on most for survival. Our nation has relinquished its divine morals, all in the name of money and capitalism. However, if we adopt a character of moral integrity, businesses and entrepreneurs alike will develop long-term relationships, and the money will follow. Simply put, having integrity requires being whole and undivided. You have to know who you are and stand for something in order to avoid reaching a breaking point at which you will compromise your soul. This may be the most challenging choice a person can face in life. However, if you have or develop integrity, then you have anything and everything you desire in this world.

**Swagger:** This simply refers to your ability to stand out from the herd. This is important in your pursuit of success and wealth creation. The ability to get people to buy into you by being yourself is often the most challenging skill to understand or acquire. Many of us think that having swag means following the herd and scorning disruption, but I don't think safety and conformity are the remedy. Having swag means that you are a trendsetter. You create your own rules, and you would rather build a company from the ground up than participate in one that is already built.

## SHOWING GRATITUDE AND PAYING HOMAGE

If you want to be fulfilled in life and in business, you have to learn to appreciate everything that you have. When you work hard at something and succeed at it, you should acknowledge that your hard work, dedication, and acumen played a pivotal role in allowing you to reach your goals. There may have been other factors that attributed to your success, such as luck, networks, and upbringing. However, the minute you stop believing in your ability to create your own success is the minute you stop working hard and things begin to be taken from you. Wealth is more about consistency and gratitude than it is about success and luck. The more you are aware of your blessings derived from your hard work, the harder you continue to work in order to maintain and preserve your accomplishments.

Showing gratitude can also come in the form of paying homage. It is okay for you to pay homage to the people you respect who have done things that you are trying to do for a long period of time and who have done them in a consistent way. Paying homage is a huge component of finding mentorship. If you are seeking mentorship from people who came before you, don't be afraid to pay homage and ask them how they were able to succeed in the area you're interested in.

Paying homage does not make you inferior to those people or anyone else, nor does it make you a people-pleaser. It shows your level of respect for the game and for the people who made the path easier for you. Now, there is a drastic difference between paying homage and glorifying a person. You earn someone's respect when you give it graciously. When you're praising people because of their fame as opposed to because you respect their work or positive impact, then that can be considered glorifying or being a fan. You get better results and respect when you compliment the people and ask questions about their work rather than complimenting them and asking questions about their fame. We are all human beings at the end of the day. They are no different than you; that's why it is vital that you respect the hustle rather than the result of it.

## PATIENCE IS A VIRTUE

The difference between fast illegal money and business money is the speed at which you recoup your investment or make money. In regard to starting your own business, it takes a very long time to set yourself free here. This is because you have to establish your brand and educate your customer base on the value proposition of your business, especially if you are entering in the start-up space. You are also forced to pay taxes on your earnings. However, if your business can sustain and survive market fluctuations and competition and you strongly believe in it and remain patient, then there can be more longevity for your business.

With fast money, you get your money back directly. However, this route will cost you significantly more than having a legitimate business will. If you go this route, you are subjected to lawsuits, prison, death, and loss of money in the long term. I do not recommend this route, as it is not only a wealth trap but a life trap.

In order to sustain anything that you do in life, it is necessary to develop patience. Don't allow society to rush you or tell you when something should work for you. Remember this is your life and other people are living in it. Instead, focus on doing honest and smart work and offering tons of value for people. In the end, you will see how going this route will reward you physically and intrinsically. Continue to set extreme goals and hustle like there is no tomorrow in order to accomplish them. However, have strong equanimity and understand that life is a marathon, not a sprint. Relax and understand that at the end of your hard work and goal setting, you will be placed where you were always destined to be.

# Financial Freedom: *My Only Hope*

## SMOKE AND MIRRORS

The first form of communication that people have with you when they see you is through your appearance. Unfortunately, in our country, appearance is so important on so many levels that it is almost impossible to get people to buy into you without having the "look." You can have all of the knowledge and answers in the world, but if you don't have the "shiny thing" that people normally gravitate to, it will be challenging for you to provide value to the world. These are not my rules, nor am I saying this is the Bible; just look at how you determine if something or someone is good for you or not. I am pretty sure that a majority of us seek out validation in the form of social currency (who or what other people admire or think is cool) or what we are taught is cool. Muhammad Ali said it best in an interview: "I need to buy the Rolls Royce, jewelry and the shiny things in order to get people to follow the gospel that I am preaching." – Muhammad Ali. We are aspirational by nature, so if we see someone who looks wealthy and accomplished, we will follow that person's word faster than we will someone who doesn't appear wealthy to our eyes.

Now, I am not saying that you have to overextend yourself or even go broke trying to have people buy into you. What I am saying is that you have to find creative ways to appeal to the masses.

Whether that is through humility, charisma, childishness, ignorance, or any other adaptation that influences the thoughts of society, leveraging this to appeal to the masses is a sure way of getting them to buy into what you are selling or promoting. My hope is that you use this strategy for good and not evil or hatred. This is how you will be able to change the world and spread the message of love and happiness for yourself and others.

## GET SHIT DONE: URGENCY

Self-explanatory! Need I say more? If you would like me to, fine. Allow me to continue. There is nothing more satisfying than sex, good credit, and getting shit done. Whether you are working on a lengthy term paper, closing on your first property, or doing your final interview, once you are able to complete the task, you begin to develop an inherent sense of pride and joy. Even if the happiness is temporary, getting stuff done is a key driver that enables you to be happy. There is a saying that goes, "Be the change you want to see in the world." This starts with getting stuff done. If you stand for something, do something constructive to show it. If you are against something, the same rules apply. If you want to begin your path to financial freedom, then work to get it done already. You gain more respect by completing a task you set out to complete than by not walking the talk, no matter how unsexy it may look or seem. We need a nation of doers, not people who pass down rhetoric like a genetic mutation. No, we need people who are walking the walk and getting shit done for the benefit of society and themselves. We need to start seeing people act on things that they stand for and put their money where their mouths are.

If you want to see more wealth equality, human ingenuity, togetherness, and innovation in your world, the world is waiting on you to get it done. Don't wait for the next person to complete the task that you set out to do. Instead, walk the walk and work hard to change the void that you see within the world, and I guarantee you that you will be happy and fulfilled beyond belief. In my opinion, this is where true purpose is hiding: in your ability to do and complete what you set out to do in the world. So my advice to you is to set a goal, a dream, or a vision and get it done no matter how it may look to someone else. We need more people who are willing to get shit done!

## YOUR PURPOSE BELONGS TO YOU—NOT ANYONE ELSE

The rise of social media and instant access to fame and acknowledgment has increased societal depression to levels unseen in human history, according to time magazine. My take is this. This global depression is a result of us trying to exist in and live someone else's purpose instead of living out our own purposes in life. We need to understand that the key to unlocking your divine gifts is to live your purpose and only yours. Your purpose is yours, and it is designed for you only! I've never before seen so many people in this world try to imitate someone else's life or do something because the media deemed it sophisticated and necessary in order to be accepted in society. Systematic depression has only been the symptom of the overall problem within humanity. The root of the problem is deeper. We are depressed not because we aren't able to measure up to the insidious demands of society but because we aren't living out our true individual purposes.

I am only saying that you have to live your purpose if you want to be admired and acknowledged. The reason is that your purpose is a kind of genius that no one else has access to. Your purpose could even be sweeping, but even if it isn't, if you are passionate about it and master it, people within that niche will admire and respect you! Whether vast or small, there is a niche for every single person on this planet. Some people have the ability to attract more people. This doesn't mean that they were given a better purpose than you; it only means that you have to find more creative ways to attract the same number of people. This is why people with no talent can have the same amount of followers as someone who is naturally gifted. Purpose has no favorites. It only works for those who discover theirs, master it, and do it better than anyone else trying to imitate what they have mastered.

You can have all the money and fame in the world and find that it's your kids who give you true purpose. The gift of purpose is a blessing that can extend through and outside of you. All you need is the right spark to ignite your true calling. It can come in many forms, including these:

- A near-death experience
- Love
- Death of a loved one
- Childbirth
- A burning desire to impact the world
- Curiosity
- One's background
- A plight or adversity
- Enlightenment

Think of more: 1._____ 2._____ 3._____

> *Learn to love yourself as much as you love someone else.*

> —*50 Cent*

You are blessed beyond measure, and your purpose is valued and needed within our society. As the R&B group TLC said, you don't have to go chasing waterfalls when your purpose is sticking to the rivers and lakes that you're used to. Instead of trying to be the next Mark Zuckerberg, Jay-Z, Beyoncé, or Barack Obama or to build the next Snapchat or Airbnb, discover your purpose by being yourself and doing what you love, even if you aren't ever acknowledged for it. This, I believe, is true purpose. So try not to worry; your purpose is inside of you. It is inside of us all. And it will constantly try to reveal itself until we finally begin to acknowledge it.

## HUMANITY'S WORK IS NOT YET FINISHED

I love starting you off with questions that will reboot your mind and get you to think profoundly and have you intensely reflect on humanity's true purpose. It is extremely important that we take time to think outside of the norm and for ourselves. Although it is critical for one's survival to learn the game of money, it is just as important to understand why we are here. Understanding this aspect of life can ease the stress that comes with your pursuit of happiness, personal success, and financial freedom. Here are a few questions we as a society should ask ourselves:

- What is humanity's true purpose?
- Are we not here to do more than just work and participate in a flawed monetary system?
- Is our purpose really to go to work every day, save, invest, and pass down money to our children, only to have this cycle repeated over and over again? Is our purpose really to achieve what is deemed personal success, such as fame and fortune, only to die and have someone else take our place?
- Why are we subjecting ourselves to animalistic and primitive states of consciousness like xenophobia, division, and manufactured social Darwinism.

The volatile current state of the world is due to human-manufactured problems. We create our problems in order to evade the truth. What is this truth, you ask? The truth is that as humanity, we are afraid of the simple fact that we are oblivious to our purpose as a group on this planet. We often try to deflect the thought of humanity's true mission on this earth. I am pretty sure that we are here for more than just to participate in a system of perceived power, money, fame, and success. I think that humanity is still in its infancy, and as we continue to evolve, we will begin to engage in our spiritual curiosity. This spiritual and collaborative curiosity will spark a unity and collaboration within all of us like nobody has ever seen before. As a result, we will finally learn why we are all here and what we are here to accomplish together.

# Final Thoughts

I wrote this book because I was inspired. What inspired me was the fact that my business experience and financial knowledge were needed among my peers and elders. I went from educating my parents about financial literacy to appearing on podcasts and panels informing my fellow millennials how to grow their wealth legally. However, I felt like I was giving out medication, not a cure. People were coming to me when they were already deep in "bad" debt with credit cards and student or car loans or after they had come across money and lost it. I was able to add value, but I felt like I was getting to people too late. So I wanted to write a book that would help people before they got into these financial debacles. I hope that you will finish this book a more enlightened person than when you started it. This is not to say that you weren't enlightened before, but I only want you to be more aware and informed about the capitalist system you currently live in. We all are part of the game of money, whether we want to play it or not. The problem lies when 1 percent of the population plays this game of money as a sport while the remaining 99 percent is forced to play the game to survive.

> *"Give a man a fish and you feed him for a day; teach a man to fish and you feed him for a lifetime."*
>
> *- CHINESE PROVERB*

The ultimate goal is to teach you how to fish so that you can establish your independence and operate out of abundance rather than fear and greed. There are enough resources in the world to go around. However, we have been conditioned to think and move like these resources are limited. I am releasing all of the information that has been stealthily and strategically kept from the masses because I want to create a new wave of financially savvy and educated people. These people will not only be financially equipped on a mental level but display a kind of empathy that will enable them to share their knowledge with someone less fortunate than they are. I believe this is the genuine meaning of social Darwinism. It is not about the survival of the fittest individual but about the survival of the most suitable humanity. We all need to learn to share our secrets if we want humanity to survive and thrive for millennia to come. Otherwise, we will continue this process of single elimination until there is no one else to eliminate, and humanity as a whole will cease to exist.

# For My Fellow Millennials

*It is not the strongest of the species that survives, nor the most intelligent, but the one most responsive to change.*

*- Charles Darwin*

Today, we are still paying for the economic party our parents and grandparents had decades ago. Although we have been hailed in many publications as the most innovative, creative, and enlightened generation in history, we are still crippled by student loan debt, underemployment, inflation, and rising home prices.

Debt has taken over our entire economic system, inflating the price of everyday goods and services. We are now forced to take on debt to survive. If we continue to save rather than put the money we have to work, our money will become worthless over time, and everyday goods and services will get more expensive. The Federal Reserve will continue to create bubbles as it increases and decreases interest rates. My advice to you is to convert your cash into an asset—something that will pay you cash flow.

# *Letter to You*

*I never noticed how intimate writing is. It almost requires a sense of vulnerability in the writer. I hate the feeling of being vulnerable. However, I love teaching, and today's climate has forced me to ignore my reclusiveness in order to share my financial knowledge with my people.We all have a spiritual and moral obligation to leave this world better than when we came into it. My job is to enlighten you and offer you as much information and value as possible to equip you with the tools necessary to compete in this game of money and in life.*

# The Everything Bubble

Stocks, bonds, and real estate

As investors in this looming global dollar debt crisis, we must understand that now is the time to leverage our cash to acquire real assets. Assets like physical gold, silver, and cash-flowing B-grade properties are all hedges against this potential economic downturn.

# Ten Keys to Success as an Entrepreneur

### 1. Have skin in the game

Invest in yourself! Build at least a minimal viable product that supports your vision or idea. It may require some capital up front, but it shows potential investors how serious you are about your idea.

### 2. Opportunity cost over financial cost

The most common reason most people struggle with building a company is cost (it's too expensive to start). Instead, look at the opportunity cost of what you stand to gain if it works or to lose if you don't start.

### 3. Always think like an investor

This means you have to forgo (delay) instant gratification for long-term gratification.

### 4. Think and scale big

In any idea or business, you discover it is often wise to look at the market on a global scale. Oftentimes our imagination is limited to our life experiences (this is why travel is one of the best investments one can make), and this limits our perspective. Instead, think about how many people there are living on earth, and go from there!

### 5. Add value

Self-explanatory...Enrich and serve people's lives, and they will pay you back for doing so.

### 6. Build a system (synergize!)

The Great Wall of China, Egypt, the Roman Empire, and the United States of America were not built by one man. They were constructed by teams of like-minded people. These systems were established because the whole was a sum of its individual parts. As the saying goes, there is no "I" in "team."

### 7. Do things that don't scale

Reach out to your customer base and the press. Get your hands dirty. And most importantly, get feedback.

### 8. Get feedback

Entrepreneurs will not know how customers are responding to their businesses unless there is user feedback. Sales and data can be indicators, but they tend to ignore long-term prospects. On the other hand, the customer can tell you what human features you can add to improve your business. This will then help to increase your bottom line.

### 9. Embrace your (personal) value proposition

Own and embrace what you (as an entrepreneur) offer, how you solve a need, and what distinguishes you from everyone else. Be confident in you!

## 10. Believe (have faith)

No one will believe in you more than yourself and God. Trust your journey. Trust the process. Understand that we all serve a purpose in this thing called life and that every life is important in the larger scheme of God's plan.

*Do you want to know a skill that is relatively fast, easy, and affordable to learn and will be in demand in the future?*

## Computer programming!

*The barrier to entry is low, and dedicated self-taught learners can make up to six figures in less than a year! Check out two dope start-ups called REWBIKS and Treehouse that are helping people learn to code without breaking the bank!*

# Allow me to query you

| Who is this? | Now who is this? |
|---|---|
| 1.  Steve Schwartzman | Jay - Z |
| 2.  David Tepper | Oprah |
| 3.  Gill Dezer | Rick Ross |
| 4.  Ray Dalio | P — Diddy |
| 5.  Reginal Lewis | Kobe Bryant |
| 6.  Van Jones | Will Smith |
| 7.  Larry Ellison | LeBron James |
| 8.  Jim & Alice Walton | Beyoncé |
| 9.  Sheldon Allison | Dr. Dre |
| 10. Jack Ma | TigerWoods |
| 11. Sheryl Sandberg | SerenaWilliams |
| 12. Carl Icahn | mike Tyson |
| 13. James Harris Simmons | Snoop Dogg |

| 14. Brian Chesky | Kevin Hart |
| 15. Erik Prince | Nicki Minaj |

*T*here is a reason why we don't know any of the people on the left column, what they do, or even how much they earn. There has been a stealthy and persistent effort to marginalize the abilities of people of color by reinforcing the stereotype of what a successful minority looks like and does. Unfortunately, the only people often shown by the media as the embodiment of success for people of color are athletes and entertainers. Although the achievements and accomplishments of the individuals on the right side of the column should be celebrated, we should understand that many other glamorous industries will enable you to produce just as much wealth as (if not more than) the sports and entertainment fields.

As you can see from the examples above, many of us only know only one side of the coin—we are aware of only one way to produce value and make money. However, the left side of the list reveals how many other passions and skills we can acquire outside of our ability to physically entertain people. This column also proves that you can still be considered a success if you aren't good at singing or balling, and you can even produce ten times the amount of wealth that you can in sports and entertainment.

# Financial Freedom: *My Only Hope*

*The best thing that money can buy is Financial Freedom*

# About the Author

J eremiah J. Brown is a serial entrepreneur, tech enthusiast, and groundbreaking product strategist. At eighteen, he became a real estate agent in his hometown of New York City. Before graduating with a degree in finance, he launched and sold his first company.

In addition to being an entrepreneur, Brown owns various properties throughout the United States. He's invested in the stock market and experienced firsthand its many ups and downs. Over time, Brown has learned to be an effective leader and to build his wealth from the bottom up.

Even before the age of thirty, he's already achieved success with multiple business ventures. He's also been featured in various publications, including Entrepreneur Magazine. Brown's entrepreneurship has allowed him to become an investor; an investor in people, and in the education of those who desire to be financially free. Despite the obstacles, Brown has shown that it is possible to achieve financial freedom in spite of any setback.

Contact Information:

Jeremiah.brwn12@gmail.com
(424) 645 7104

Printed in Great Britain
by Amazon